FASTBALL FITNESS:

The Art and Science of Training to Throw with Real Velocity

Tom House, Ph.D.

**Foreword By
Dr. Tim Kremchek
Chief Orthopedic Surgeon,
Cincinnati Reds Baseball Organization**

**COACHES
CHOICE** ™

ISBN: 978-1-58518-037-0
Library of Congress Control Number: 2007921662
Cover design: Studio J Art & Design
Book layout: Studio J Art & Design
Front cover photo: Joe Patronite/Getty Images Sport

Coaches Choice
P.O. Box 1828
Monterey, CA 93942
www.coacheschoice.com

It is a privilege to write the foreword for Tom House's book, *Fastball Fitness: The Art and Science of Training to Throw with Real Velocity*. Like Tom and millions around the world, I love the game of baseball and want to make it a better and safer game for those who play it. Tom has taken the art of pitching and made it a lifetime passion. As a player, to a coach, educator, researcher, and author, he has a passion for the game of baseball and a thirst to understand what makes a pitcher better. Tom has spent his life trying to understand and research the art and science of pitching, not only to make players perform better but pitch without an undue risk of being injured. Tom has also expended considerable energy attempting to determine what it takes for a pitcher to come back from an injury and pitch to a high level.

The book dispels and contradicts some of the traditional thinking of pitching mechanics and strength and conditioning methods for optimal performance pitching. Tom has uncovered the importance of rotational momentum in pitching velocity and validated this discovery through research models. He has developed methods of unique functional strengthening and conditioning for the thrower that allows performance at the highest level possible. The book also outlines conditioning methods to develop arm strength and speed through innovative throwing methods. Understanding the mechanics of pitching a baseball can be difficult, but Tom has made this factor easy to understand in a common sense manner.

As an orthopedic surgeon who specializes in sports medicine and throwers' injuries and also has a love for the game of baseball, I am impressed with the thought process, the research, and the passion put forth in this book to make the art of pitching better and safer for all who participate. I have a much deeper understanding of what allows a pitcher to have better velocity and to be more effective. I will recommend all of my coaches and parents read this book to help their players and children be better, healthier athletes and enjoy the great game of baseball.

Timothy E. Kremchek, MD
Chief Orthopedic Surgeon
Cincinnati Reds Baseball Organization

Foreword

Contents

The newly researched fastball information and instruction presented in this book are the result of collaboration between individuals from seven distinct entities:

❑ Tom House, Ph.D., The National Pitching Association (NPA), San Diego, California

❑ Eric Andrews, B.S., The National Pitching Association (NPA), San Diego, California

❑ Eric Barajas, M.A., Pacific Athletic Club of San Diego

❑ Troy Merckle, P.T., Beacon Orthopedics/Champion Sports, Cincinnati, Ohio

❑ Greg Rose, Ph.D., The Titleist Performance Institute (TPI), Carlsbad, California

❑ Simon Webb, P.T., Victoria Institute of Sport, Melbourne, Australia

❑ Mike Paul, Elite Baseball Academy, Grand Rapids, Michigan

❑ Alan Tyson, P.T., OrthoCarolina

The organizations with which these six individuals are affiliated represent some of baseball's best contemporary resources for state-of-the-art coaching science, exercise science, medical science, and/or computer science. More importantly, the people involved in this collaboration are truly committed to seeking out science-based, objective research to support and reinforce sound pitching information and instruction.

In the process of this collaborative effort, some very interesting discoveries occurred. For example, the motion analysis data on the golf swing (from TPI) and motion analysis data on a pitcher's delivery had remarkable kinematic and kinetic energy similarities for both performance and health. Furthermore, it was discovered that the physical assessment and training protocols for developing strength, endurance, and flexibility for golfers, hitters, throwers, and strikers were quite similar. As a result, where pertinent, several throwing/striking kinematics and conditioning from golf and football, as well as baseball, are illustrated side by side, throughout the manuscript. This design factor helps facilitate a better understanding about how throwers and strikers must prepare and use their bodies to generate maximum velocity with a club, a bat, or a ball.

Almost without exception, all pitchers want to throw harder. Every professional scout or college recruiter will tell anyone who asks that 90 mph is a magic number. In turn, every baseball coach, broadcaster, and sportswriter has a standard conventional-wisdom opinion to describe how pitchers generate fastball velocity. Traditionally, to be kind, baseball has been a game of failure

Introduction

coached by negative individuals in a misinformation environment. Unfortunately, a lot of fiction and not enough real fact about pitchers and how they should throw a fastball exist. The pages in this book present new, science-based research about the velocity of a thrown pitch. The primary goal of this book is to help pitchers and coaches maximize fastball performance and minimize the risk of injury. In that regard, three critical factors are addressed in the text:

- Velocity *assessment* for quantifying the contribution of rotational momentum and directional momentum on real velocity
- Velocity *evaluation* for illustrating and explaining the interaction of biomechanics, functional strength, and timing on real velocity
- Velocity *enhancement* for integrating cross-specific 1) bio-mechanically efficient skill training protocols to improve energy sequencing, arm speed, totally body strength/flexibility, and real velocity, 2) rotational strength/endurance/flexibility training protocols, and 3) under/over loading implement weight-training protocols.

ROTATIONAL MOMENTUM, DIRECTIONAL MOMENTUM, TIMING, AND FASTBALL VELOCITY

With a pitcher, velocity can be viewed in three distinct ways: 1) *real* velocity or the actual MPH "read" on a radar gun, 2) *perceived* velocity or what distance traveled and deception does to the way a pitched baseball is "read" by a hitter, and 3) *effective* velocity or how a previous pitch's speed and location affects a hitter's read on the next pitch's speed and location. Real velocity is genetic. Pitchers are born with a biological speed limit that cannot be exceeded no matter how biomechanically efficient or how functionally strong they become with training. The initial findings of the collaborative effort indicate that most pitchers compete at a sub-optimal velocity level.

This book was written to update the baseball community on current science-based research that was undertaken to facilitate a better understanding about 1) how a pitcher develops and maintains efficient mechanics, and 2) how he can condition himself to deliver a baseball with his genetically optimal real velocity, as close to home plate as possible, for added perceived velocity. In this regard, one of the goals of the research was to determine exactly what generates real velocity in a delivery. To accomplish this objective, valid, reliable testing and teaching protocols had to be developed.

We chose to isolate and measure the contribution of hip/shoulder separation/rotation to real velocity by measuring ball speeds from the NPA 2-knee drill. The reasons for this decision were quite simple. Putting a pitcher on both knees allowed us to 1) minimize and/or eliminate any directional weight shift, and 2) isolate and measure degrees of hip/shoulder separation and rotation for correlation with maximum ball velocity on each throw. After quantifying a pitcher's maximum velocity from his knees, he then moved to a mound to throw, using his actual delivery. Since pitchers can move farther, faster *directionally* when they stride *down a hill* than when they move/stride on *flat ground*, the conventional wisdom surrounding hard throwers surmised that velocity was derived by maximizing "leg drive" down the mound.

Imagine the surprise when all the numbers revealed that a larger percent of real velocity came from a pitcher's rotational momentum, *not* his directional momentum. At this point, it can help to paint a picture or two that illustrate what now seems quite obvious, but didn't before our various studies.

Visualize track and field athletes performing the hammer throw and the shot put. As implements, a hammer and a shot put weigh about the same. The hammer thrower moves forward (directional momentum) with violent spinning (rotational momentum) and throws the hammer farther than a shot putter who tosses the shot with a hopping weight shift from back foot to front foot (directional momentum), while twisting and torquing his hips/shoulders (rotational momentum). Both tosses have highly explosive rotational and directional components. On the other hand, when pinpoint accuracy isn't as important as distance, timing a throw to employ more rotational momentum rather than directional momentum will create a longer throw.

Next, visualize a slingshot and trying to hit a target *accurately*. Basically, two types of slingshots exist: 1) a David-and-Goliath slingshot that spins in a circle before the release mechanism is unleashed (rotational momentum), and 2) a traditional wrist-rocket that stretches rubber/medical tubing straight back and snaps straight, thereby contracting back and unleashing the release mechanism (directional momentum). Clearly, a David-and-Goliath slingshot generates more velocity with rotation than a wrist-rocket slingshot does with direction. On the other hand, a David-and-Goliath slingshot requires better timing and more skill to be used accurately.

At this point, put those slingshot thoughts on hold and visualize throwing darts. Very little, if any, rotational momentum occurs when you throw a dart at a target, just nonviolent, perfectly timed, precision-implemented skill, using directional momentum generated by the forearm, wrist, and hand to deliver the dart as accurately as possible.

Finally, visualize a pitcher delivering a baseball down a mound, trying to hit a catcher's glove—an 8-inch circle approximately 54 feet away. The task is both rotational and directional. To throw hard and accurately, the pitcher must maximize and efficiently time his rotational momentum with his directional momentum to optimize the energy translation coming from first his feet, then to his fingertips, and finally out onto the baseball. It's all about angles, distance, and time. If he puts too much rotation on the ball, he will have maximum real velocity but poor command of the pitch. With too much direction, he will have improved command of the pitch but a sub-optimal level of real velocity. With poorly timed rotation and direction, the pitcher will not only have sub-optimal velocity and a lack of command, but also increased stress on his joints and injury issues. In other words, coaches ask pitchers to both *time* and *sequence* the rotational violence/momentum of a hammer thrower with the directional precision/momentum of a dart thrower. Frankly, these descriptions of the pitching motion made sense to us. Hopefully, going forward, they will make sense to the baseball community.

The next step in our research and development progression was to conduct tests to validate the timing, velocity, and efficiency of our rotation/direction ratios. Subsequently, when the data from each individual velocity study was combined, the aggregate numbers revealed that in an efficiently timed delivery, a pitcher's hip/shoulder separation and delayed shoulder rotational momentum account for 80% of his real velocity. A pitcher's stride with spine/torso extension/flexion and directional momentum account for the other 20% of his real velocity. Chart S1-3 illustrates the functional derivation of real velocity, based on research involving the determination of real velocities for 200 pitchers with 1) rotational momentum *only*, on knees/flat ground, and 2) a combination of rotational momentum and directional momentum on feet/mound.

THE STUDY

This section provides an overview of the key steps involved in conducting the study. Three main areas are addressed: data collection, results, and what the results mean.

❑ Data Collection (recording the velocities):
  • When throwing from their knees, pitchers were instructed to initially start with a knee position near 45 degrees to the target.
  • Pitchers were encouraged to try increasing and/or decreasing the angle during practice throws to find an angle with which they were most comfortable.
  • If a pitcher felt at first he was "throwing across his body too much," he was encouraged to increase the angle of his knees (shoulders becoming more "square" to the target) until he felt more comfortable.
  • If a pitcher felt at first he was "too open" during his practice throws, he was encouraged to decrease the angle (glove-side shoulder facing more toward the target) until he felt more comfortable or until he felt he was throwing harder.
  • Once the position in which the player was most comfortable and throwing the hardest from was determined, the hip/knee angle was noted with the use of a "knee mat" that we developed in order to measure angles of separation. The mat (basically a large protractor) also allowed us to measure how far each player brought his throwing shoulder back; the two measures of angles allowed us to measure each player's "degree of hip and shoulder separation."

✓ Previous research conducted by various pitching coaches and performance analysts in recent years and in some cases with the help of three-dimensional motion analysis indicated that most elite pitchers get between 40 and 60 degrees of hip/shoulder separation.

✓ In our study, we had a player whose optimal hip angle was 25 degrees. He brought his arm back only five degrees, giving him a total of 30 degrees of hip and shoulder separation. Obviously, he "had more in the tank." Another player in our study was most efficient at 45 degrees on his knees. He brought his arm back 15 degrees, giving him a total of 60 degrees hip and shoulder separation.

• Pitchers were asked, while in the knee position, to slightly lean forward in order to maintain dynamic balance and to stabilize their posture. We also asked them to "sit down" a little bit in order to decrease the distance from their rear ends to their feet—basically lowering their center of gravity. They started with their hands in a relaxed manner (just as they would hold their hands together on the mound) and were encouraged to take their arm back in the same manner, speed, and direction as they normally would when delivering a pitch from the mound. In other words, they were asked to throw with their regular pitching mechanics while they were in the knee-drill position.

• The same "JUGS" model radar gun was used to record all velocities during the study.

• After originally experimenting with the radar gun in different locations, it was decided to position the gun directly behind (three or four feet) the pitcher's throwing arm in order to capture the velocity at exit speed.

• The same procedures were followed when recording pitch velocities for throws made off the pitching mound.

• Other than the initial setup, no instruction about mechanics was given when capturing velocities from flat ground/knees or from mound/full delivery.

• Pitchers were encouraged to throw as hard as they could, while maintaining what they understood to be proper mechanics in both positions.

• After each pitcher finished throwing, his data was reviewed in an effort to help him learn and improve. Discussions included coach/pitcher quantification of the most efficient hip angle for doing the knee drill, as well as the proper level of hip and shoulder separation during the pitching motion (specific to that particular pitcher).

❑ Study Results:

The first number (AVG) in the following player results represents the overall speed differential (AVG fastball velocity from mound minus AVG velocity from knees) among all players in that particular age group. The MAX represents the highest differential in the age group, while the MIN represents the smallest differential among the group. The MODE is the number representing the speed differential that showed up most often in that group. The second AVG shown represents the overall AVG velocity percentage that occurred from throwing from their knees. The MAX illustrates the highest percentage of velocity that came from the knees for the age group; MIN represents the least percentage of velocity that came from the movement represented by throwing from the knees. The second MODE represents the percentage that showed up most frequently for that age group.

Youth: Final Analysis of All Players in This Group (31 Pitchers)
- AVG 13.93 mph (the AVG speed differential for all players in this group; AVG mph from mound minus AVG mph from knees)
- MAX = 21 mph (best fastball from the mound minus the worst velocity from the knees by a player in this group)
- MIN = 9 mph (best fastball from the mound minus the best velocity from the knees by a player in this group)
- MODE = 12 mph (differential between mound velocity and knee velocity that occurred most often for all players in this group)
- AVG = 77.19% (AVG % of velocity that occurred by throwing from the knees for all players in this group)
- MAX = 83% (highest AVG % of velocity that occurred by throwing from the knees from a player in this group)
- MIN = 68% (lowest AVG % of velocity that occurred by throwing from the knees from a player in this group)
- MODE = 82% (% that occurred most often in this age group)

High School: Final Analysis of All Players in This Group (69 Pitchers)
- AVG 14.65 mph
- MAX = 21 mph
- MIN = 11 mph
- MODE = 14 mph
- AVG = 79.84%
- MAX = 86%
- MIN = 72%
- MODE = 82%

College: Final Analysis of All Players in This Group (52 Pitchers)
- AVG 15.94 mph
- MAX = 23 mph
- MIN = 10 mph
- MODE = 17 mph
- AVG = 80%
- MAX = 86%
- MIN = 72%
- MODE = 80%

<u>Professional: Final Analysis of All Players in This Group (48 Pitchers)</u>

- AVG 16.67 mph
- MAX = 22 mph
- MIN = 17 mph
- MODE N/A
- AVG = 79.67%
- MAX = 84%
- MIN = 73%
- MODE = 81%

❏ What the Numbers Mean:

- Many pitching coaches have ideas about where velocity is generated from during the pitching motion. Some believe it comes from generating "torque" in the upper body, others by "scapular loading." Still others believe in the more conventional wisdom—throwing hard comes from using the legs, having a very high leg lift, or from "pushing off the rubber."

- The results from our study indicate that just about 80% of a pitcher's real velocity comes from the torque of hip and shoulder separation; more specifically, the rotational, not linear, sequence of the pitching delivery. The averages from all ages and skill levels are very close to one another; too close in our opinion to be "coincidence."

- When the athletes threw from their knees, they had no legs involved in the throwing motion, no slope from a mound to gain momentum from, and no leg lift to generate power and/or increase potential energy. It was determined that the derived energy or potential to increase momentum from all these factors only contributed to roughly 20% of total velocity from pitches on the mound.

- The MIN and MAX (speed differential) were similar across all age groups and skill levels. As a general rule, the least amount of velocity a pitcher was going to gain by going to the mound (after throwing from his knees) was 10 mph. The most velocity a player gained by engaging in a similar scenario was about 22 mph. The AVG came to 15 mph when considering all age groups and skill levels. Essentially, the velocities from an athlete throwing from his knees can be recorded, the average computed, 15 mph added to it, and we can come extremely close to predicting what his overall velocity will be when he throws pitches from the mound.

- The MIN and MAX (percentage of velocity that came from hip/shoulder separation alone) were also very similar. Across the board, the least amount of velocity the pitchers could generate from hip/shoulder separation was roughly 71%. The highest percentage for all age groups and skill levels was roughly 84%. In summary, it can be safely stated that 71-84% of the pitcher's velocity came from the rotational energy sequence—not the directional sequence. These were the extremes, given that the average for each group and all pitchers collectively was 80%.

- In our opinion, factors such as maximizing the efficiency of leg lift, maximizing momentum, and having a strong lower body are essential to maximizing velocity and linear momentum during the pitching delivery. However, we are now convinced that most of a pitcher's velocity does not come from these areas, rather it comes from other sources—specifically hip/shoulder separation.
- By finding the optimal level of torque and maximizing the hip and shoulder separation of a pitcher (while keeping balance and posture throughout the delivery), we believe a pitcher's velocity can be increased.
- In this regard, the most effective approach to enhancing a pitcher's delivery includes the following steps:
  - ✓ Understanding and accepting the validity of new, objective information.
  - ✓ Incorporating specific drills into a pitcher's workouts that support the new information.
  - ✓ Introducing a training routine specific to the torso and core in order to improve rotational strength and flexibility. This step will allow for better, more efficient hip and shoulder separation/rotation during the pitching delivery.
- An understanding that hip and shoulder separation/rotation is the primary source of velocity points out how important *timing* is to an efficient delivery. As such, the rotational part of a pitcher's delivery demands perfect timing for maximizing velocity.
- An "in-depth" discussion of the biomechanical derivation and timing of real velocity is presented in Chapter 1.

1

The Biomechanical Derivation of Real Velocity: Fact, Fiction, Contradiction, Paradox, and Paradigm Shifts

(Tom House and Eric Andrews)

The discussion and data on momentum and velocity that was addressed in Section I provide a better understanding about the contributions of hip/shoulder rotation and total body/torso direction to real fastball velocity. This chapter examines the impact of timing, along with the progression of critical events and the biomechanical variables involved in an efficient delivery, on real velocity. This factor is important because the more that is understood about a pitcher's delivery, the more capable coaches will be to physically prepare a pitcher's body to use the proper delivery and perform at his best in competition.

The 80%-20% rotational quantifications make more sense when Graph 1-1 is examined. As this graph shows, the pitcher's hips can rotate with an angular velocity of 750-1000° per second (25-30 mph). Furthermore, this pitcher's shoulders can rotate with an angular velocity of 1000-1250° per second (30-35 mph), while his forearm can internally rotate with an angular velocity of 2500-3000° per second (65-75 mph). Chart 1-1 illustrates that when timing the progression of critical events with key variables in a pitcher's delivery, this pitcher's total body/torso can only move forward into foot strike with low back/spine extension, firing into low back/spine flexion at approximately six feet per second (four mph). However, when the kinematic sequencing of these rotational/directional momentums are timed properly, the summation of forces translate kinetic energy from feet to fingertips and out onto the baseball, actually "cracking the whip" for this pitcher's fastball, between 90-95 mph.

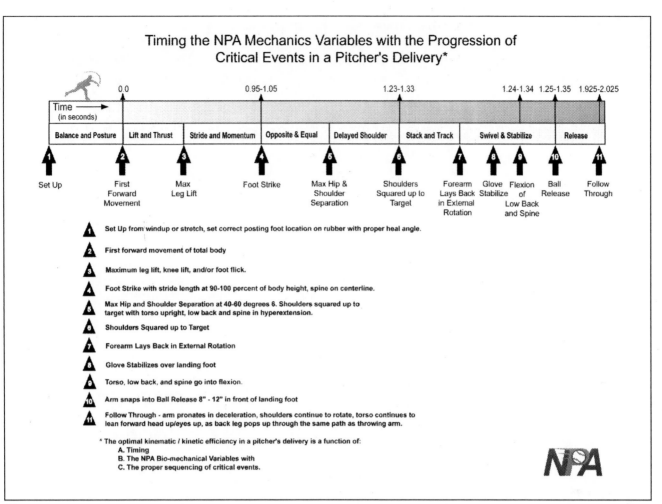

Chart 1-1

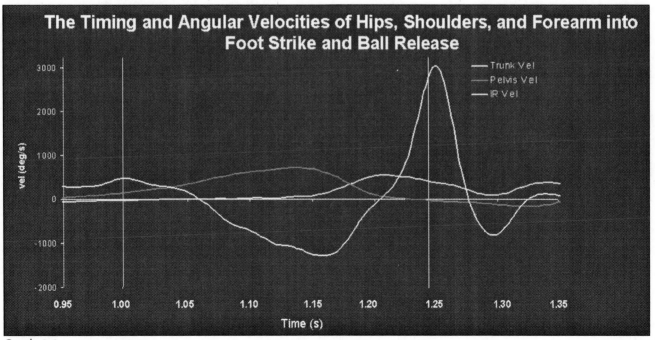

Graph 1-1

These measurements and quantifications have exciting implications. Being excited about something new, however, isn't enough. It's also necessary to identify what information already exists about the factors that affect the velocity of a fastball and try to separate fact from fiction and contradiction, as well as identify paradox and paradigm shifts.

Our research collaboration has revealed the following statements to be fastball fiction:

- Pitching is an unnatural movement.
- Velocity is maximized when a pitcher stays back, stops at the top, and doesn't rush.
- Velocity is improved when stride and mechanics are linear.
- Velocity is improved by scapular loading.
- Velocity is increased by pulling glove to chest.
- Velocity is maximized with a longer throwing arm path.
- Velocity is improved by getting on top.
- Four-seam fastballs are faster than two-seam fastballs.
- Velocity is improved with power-lifting protocols.

Furthermore, our research collaboration supports the following statements as fastball *fact*:

- The mound is the only unnatural thing about pitching (humans are designed to move on flat ground).
- Pitchers are throwers by species (somebody in every pitcher's ancestry probably threw rocks at rabbits to eat).
- Pitchers are born with a genetic governor on how hard they can throw and will never throw harder than their genetic predisposition.
- Most pitchers suboptimize their genetic predisposition for fastball velocity.
- A pitcher's head and spine must stay balanced and *behind* the center of gravity during weight transfer and stride into foot strike to maximize fastball velocity.
- A pitcher's spine/torso must stay upright and hyperextended until his shoulders square up to the target for maximum fastball velocity.
- A pitcher's torso must track to a stable glove, as throwing his forearm lays back into external rotation to optimize fastball velocity.
- A pitcher's spine/torso must move into flexion just before his throwing forearm snaps straight into ball release for maximum velocity.
- A pitcher's grip is secondary to the angle of wrist and forearm when it comes to maximizing fastball velocity.
- A pitcher's scapulars do not preload for velocity.
- Scapular loading takes place after foot strike, not before landing foot contact. This loading occurs eccentrically during the hip/shoulder separation and the delayed shoulder rotation phase of the delivery.

- A pitcher's arm path is unique to his delivery. When "mirrored" with his glove-side arm, it facilitates the timing of his throw.
- In an efficient delivery, a pitcher's stride length, direction, and landing foot position are biomechanically inevitable.
- Velocity is optimized when the pitcher's legs allow weight transfer and stride to go further faster. (It should be noted that primitive humans didn't "stay back" or "stop at the top" when they were throwing rocks at those rabbits.)
- Strength and flexibility training for a further, faster stride actually facilitate the *timing* of a pitcher's kinematics and a more efficient progression of critical events.
- For optimal timing in a delivery, a pitcher (of any age) should weight shift and stride into front foot contact in ~1 second or less. The rest of the body takes ~.25 seconds to deliver the pitch and .65 seconds to decelerate the arm after the pitch is delivered.
- A pitcher's maximum fastball velocity has a unique kinematic "signature" that involves the feet-to-fingertip *timing* of kinetic energy, generated by an efficient kinematic *sequencing of directional momentum* and *rotational momentum*.

In addition, our research collaboration supports the following paradoxes about pitching:
- Posting foot position/angle facilitates the timing of biomechanical variables.
- No matter what posture a pitcher starts in, his body will find a posture he is strong enough to maintain throughout his delivery. (Note in Figures 1-1 to 1-3, the head drops down during delivery, while in Figures 1-4 to 1-6 the head pops up during delivery.)
- Moving faster facilitates the sequencing of critical events.
- The longer a pitcher takes to get into foot strike, the stronger he needs to be.
- The longer a pitcher takes to get into foot strike, the more things that can go wrong with his delivery.
- Stride length is affected by the functional strength and the weight of the pitcher's throwing implement (towel, weighted ball, regular ball, etc.).
- Stride length is affected by keeping the foot off the ground longer in the same (one second) foot-strike timeframe.
- Arm-path length is affected by functional strength and the weight of the pitcher's throwing implement (towel, weighted ball, regular ball, etc.).
- Most hard throwers have "short-arm" paths. (More arm speed = more arm stress and requires more strength and stability.)

One exercise that we use to teach the proper timing of a pitcher's body mechanics is the towel drill. As Figures 1-7 to 1-9 illustrate, not only will a pitcher stride further with a towel than a baseball, his arm path will also be slightly longer when throwing a towel, rather than a baseball.

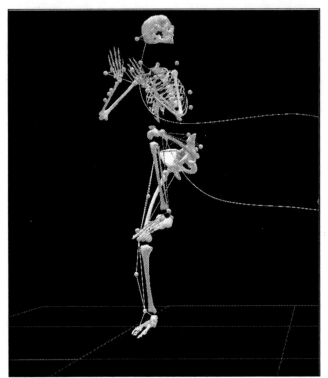

Figure 1-1

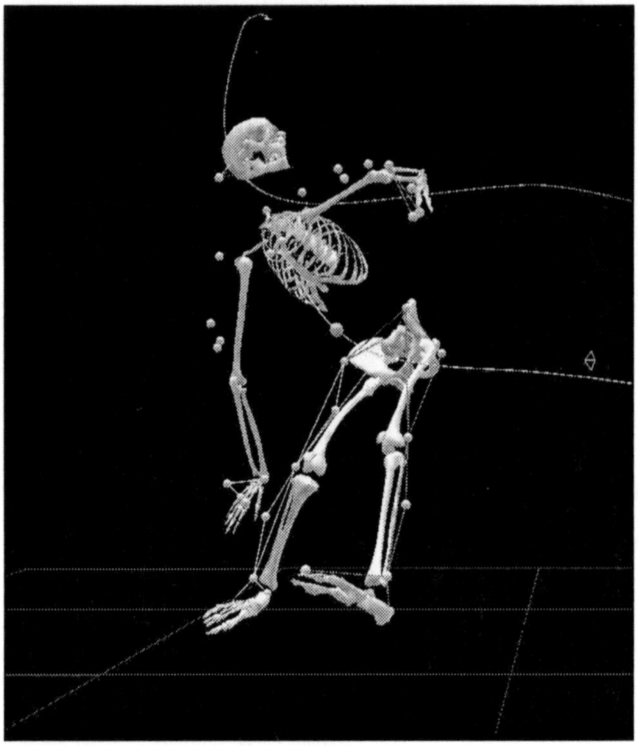

Figure 1-2

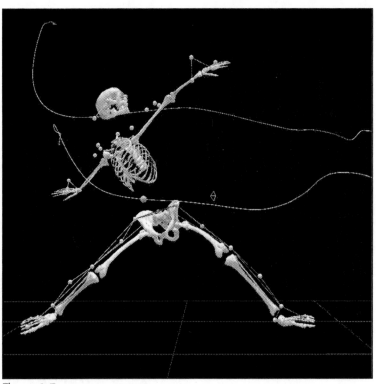

Figure 1-3

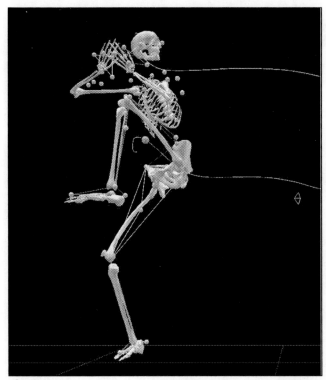

Figure 1-4

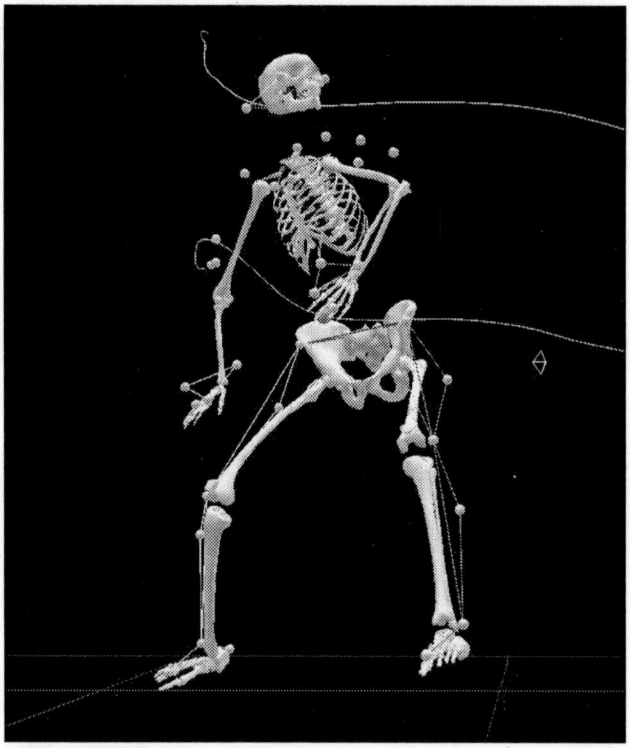

Figure 1-5

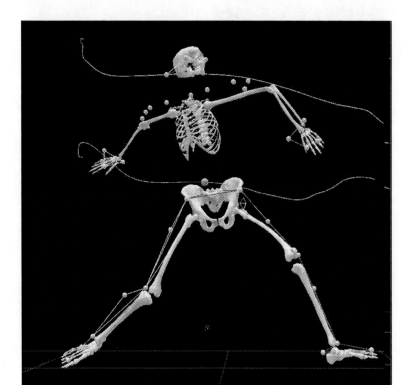

Figure 1-6

Towel Drill vs. Baseball

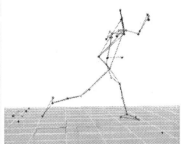

Figure 1-7   Figure 1-8   Figure 1-9

Purpose: To teach the proper timing of body mechanics. (It should be noted that it is NOT a release-point drill).

Key points:
- Matches rotational & directional momentum
- Motion analysis shows that the towel drill has the same biomechanical signature as pitching a baseball, with the following exceptions:
  ✓ A pitcher will stride further with a towel than with a baseball (note the stride length above)
  ✓ Arm path is slightly longer with a towel than with a baseball
- The towel drill puts minimal stress on the throwing arm because the towel weighs less than a baseball

Having gained a better understanding about what contributes (biomechanically) to real velocity, the next step is to examine how the legs, torso, and spine contribute to a pitcher's real velocity (Chapters 2-4). It should be noted that the contribution of the throwing arm to real velocity is not discussed until Section IV.

2

How the Legs Contribute to the Mechanics of Real Velocity

A pitcher's legs are the foundation of his weight transfer. They are also the support for his kinematic sequencing for optimizing the rotational movements and the integrated movement of his joints/extremities. Figure 2-1 illustrates the sequencing. As such, they affect his kinetic energy translation, which maximizes the amount of energy getting through the body from his feet to his fingertips, and eventually out onto the baseball. It is important to emphasize that the efficient use of the legs sets up efficient biomechanical kinematics and the timing of kinetic energy created by directional and rotational momentum. The velocity of the ball is optimized when a pitcher's…:

- Torso/posture is maintained by posting foot/leg and landing foot/leg during weight transfer.
- Posting foot/back leg flexes, firms up, stabilizes, and loads (isometrically and eccentrically) during front leg lift.
- Butt moves aggressively forward to initiate weight transfer and stays in front of a stable head/spine/center of gravity posture, into front foot contact. The back leg never straightens; as…
- Stride moves the body, directionally, on a straight, closed, or open line as far and as fast as possible, into front-foot contact. How far is determined by the speed of the weight transfer, the pitcher's level of functional strength and flexibility, and his skill to keep his front foot off the ground as long as possible (inside the one second weight shift parameter). The head/spine stay upright, and the torso tracks naturally; as…

A well-designed health assessment or medical history questionnaire can identify most medical conditions, symptoms, and risk factors that are predictive of future cardiovascular disease or medical conditions.

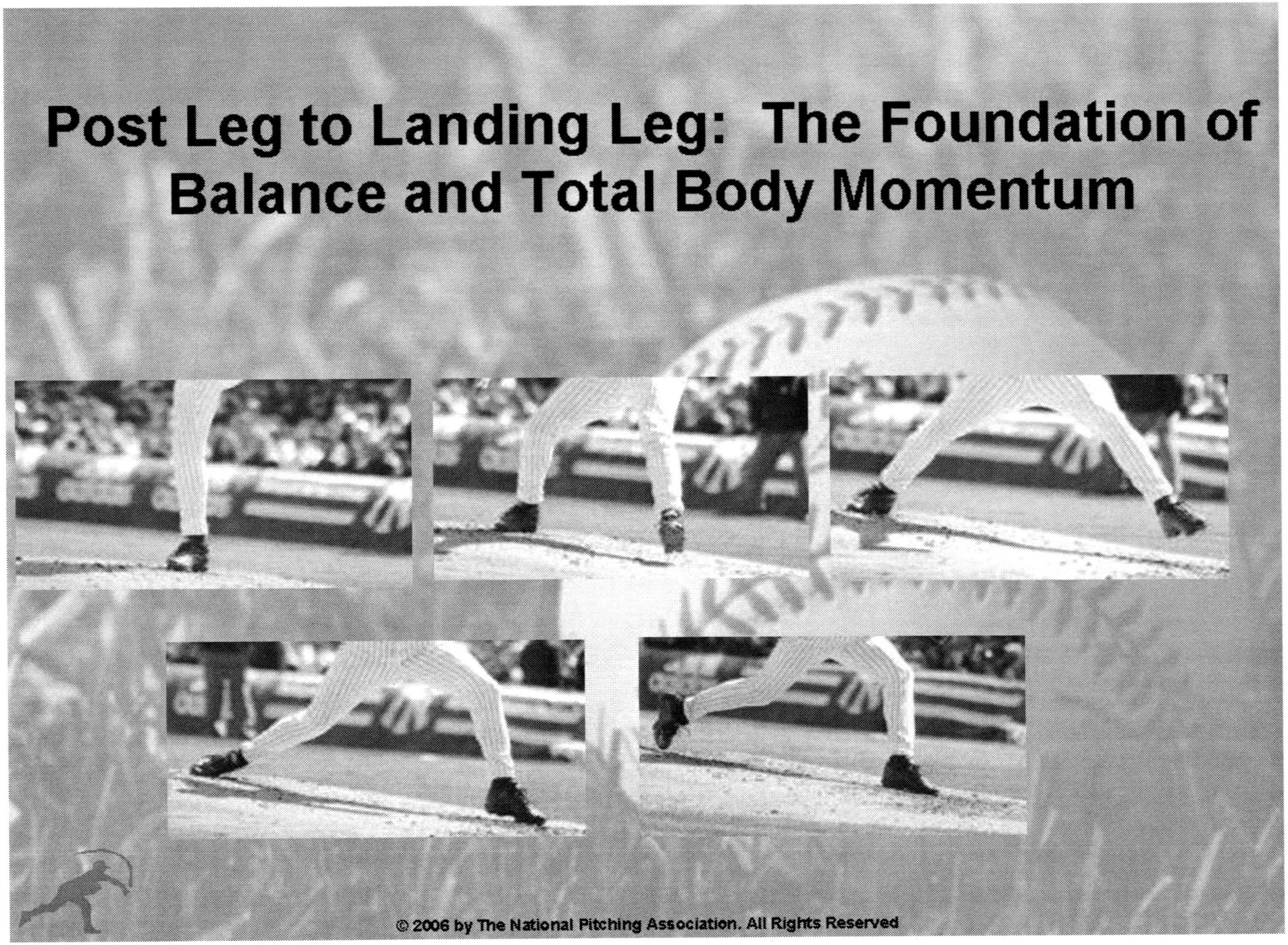
Post Leg to Landing Leg: The Foundation of Balance and Total Body Momentum
© 2006 by The National Pitching Association. All Rights Reserved

Figure 2-1

- The landing leg flexes, firms up, and stabilizes isometrically into 110-90° of knee flexion, as…
    - ✓ His glove swivels and stabilizes over the front foot, while the upright torso continues to move forward toward a stable glove, over the front foot.
    - ✓ Hips/shoulders maintain 40-60° of separation, sequentially rotating as late as his strength/flexibility will allow, squaring up to the target, as the throwing forearm lays back in external rotation, while the total body slows to deliver the arm/ball into the release point.
    - ✓ Back foot/leg drags on the center line and comes off the ground at the ball release, popping up for balance during the follow-through, in the same slot as the throwing-arm went through to delivery the ball.

An inherent need exists for conditioning coaches to understand the mechanics of the legs in the pitcher's delivery. Training for useable strength/endurance to support range of motion with functional stability, mobility, and/or flexibility, cross specific to pitching, requires a paradigm shift. For example, examine the two basic lifts involved with traditional olympic/power lifting—the squat and the bench press. Any benefits achieved by training to perform a squat are outweighed by the risks involved in doing the exercise. Why? While the squat exercise might be good for muscle, it's bad for the knee joints and low back. Furthermore, training to perform the squat occurs on two feet, while a pitcher is always on one foot or the other while throwing. Finally, the squat does not involve rotation training, which is where 80% of a pitcher's velocity comes from. The same argument can be advanced against the bench press: good for muscle; hard on shoulder and elbow joints; involves training with two hands for a pitcher who is always moving a ball and a glove with one hand; and no torso rotation is involved.

Consequently, a lot of functional movement, closed-chain resistance training for the legs, like straight and side lunge work (with torso twists), is included in the training protocols detailed in this book. The contribution of the hips and shoulders to real velocity is discussed in the next chapter.

3

How the Hips and Shoulders Contribute to the Mechanics of Real Velocity

As was previously discussed, our research has indicated that 80% of real velocity is generated by rotational momentum of the hips and shoulders. In that regard, fastball velocity is maximized when…:

- The hips/shoulders separate between 40-60° around an upright, hyper-extended, low back/spine. Pitchers can create these angles with big hip/small shoulder rotation, equal hip/shoulder rotation, or small hip/big shoulder rotations (Figure 3-1).

- The hips/shoulders maintain their degree of separation as long as the pitcher's strength/flexibility will allow his total body to track forward toward a firm landing leg and a stable glove positioned over the landing foot in front of the torso.

- The throwing shoulder delays rotation until the hips have slowed/stopped their rotation. An elite pitcher's throwing shoulder doesn't start rotating forward until the spine has tracked 75%-80% of stride length.

- Scapular "loading" occurs as an unconscious accommodation to help the throwing shoulder stabilize and compensate for the weight of the throwing arm/baseball. A maximum eccentric load is imposed when the throwing shoulder changes direction, while the throwing forearm begins to lay back into "external rotation."

Scapular loading is biomechanically inevitable. Trying to instruct scapular loading can cause inefficiently timed kinematic sequencing and/or inefficient kinetic energy translation (i.e., premature frontside rotation and/or recruiting strength out of sequence). Coincidentally, the hip/shoulder separation and scapular loading of a pitcher (Figure 3-2) is exactly the same as the hips/shoulder separation and scapular loading of a golfer (Figure 3-3). Golfers refer to this phenomenon as the "X" factor, while baseball pitchers call it torque. In either sport, the best athletes create and maintain the most separation.

Having addressed how hip and shoulder kinematics, sequencing, and timing contribute to real velocity in a pitcher's delivery, the next step is to examine how the spine and torso affect real velocity.

Figure 3-1

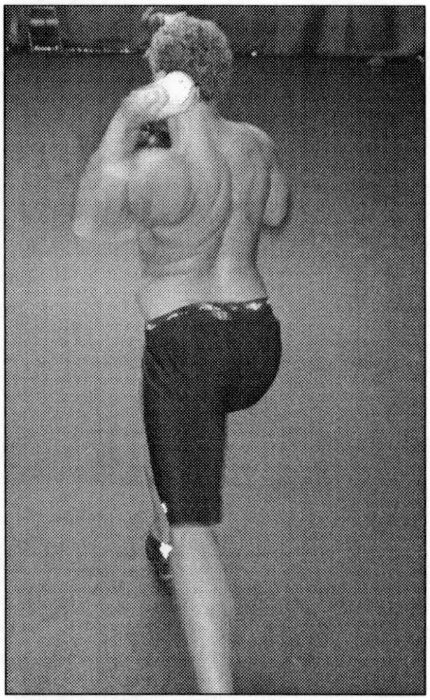

Figure 3-2

Figure 3-3

4

How the Spine and Torso Contribute to the Mechanics of Real Velocity

As was previously discussed, our research has indicated that 20% of ball velocity is generated by directional momentum. In turn, fastball velocity is maximized when aggressive movement occurs on the same straight, closed, open stride line as a pitcher's…:

- Total body tracks with an upright head and spine in a weight shift from the posting foot to landing foot (Figure 4-1).
- Low back/spine hyperextends to keep the torso upright and stacked, while the hip/shoulders separate, delay rotation, square up, and track into a flexed and firm front leg (Figure 4-2).
- Glove swivels and stabilizes over his front foot, while his throwing arm lays back in external rotation (Figure 4-2).
- Low back/spine go from hyperextension to flexion just before his throwing forearm snaps straight from external rotation into internal rotation and the release point (Figures 4-3 and 4-4).

Similar to the impact of the hips and shoulders, it's interesting to note that the spine/torso (stack and track) of a pitcher throwing a baseball does the same thing as the spine/torso (squat thrusts) of a golfer swinging a club. Figure 4-5 illustrates the point.

Given the availability of data on real velocity assessment and evaluation, an obvious question arises concerning whether it is possible to train and enhance the physical/biomechanical contribution of rotational momentum and/or directional momentum to the velocity of a fastball. The answer is a resounding yes. In our collaborative research, we discovered that cross-specific training for *rotational* strength/endurance/flexibility is the safest, most effective way to create fastball velocity.

This finding is an obvious departure from traditional power-based training and/or speed and quickness training protocols. This departure leads into the rotational, strength, endurance, and flexibility training discussion in Section II: "THE PREHABILITATION TRAINING REGIMENS FOR ROTATIONAL MOMENTUM, DIRECTIONAL MOMENTUM, AND FASTBALL VELOCITY."

Figure 4-1

Figure 4-2

Figure 4-3

Figure 4-4

Low-Back Extension

Directional Momentum in a
Pitcher's Weight Transfer
(Stack & Track)

Directional Momentum in a Golfer's Weight Transfer
(Squat Thrust)

Low-Back Flexion

Figure 4-5

PREHABILITATION TRAINING REGIMENS FOR ROTATIONAL MOMENTUM, DIRECTIONAL MOMENTUM, AND FASTBALL VELOCITY

The first section of *Fastball Fitness* discussed new information and instruction about the contribution of rotational biomechanics and kinematic timing to kinetic energy sequencing and fastball velocity. This new research forced a paradigm shift in the way we believe that pitchers should be conditioned to support the physical stresses imposed on their body by their competitive workloads. The second section of this text examines the what, where, why, and how we have altered traditional resistance-training protocols to functionally address *rotational* strength, endurance, and flexibility, as well as *directional* strength, endurance and flexibility for real velocity.

Our efforts to determine the most effective training protocols for pitchers initially involved identifying the physical contributions of a pitcher's legs, core, and arms to a delivery. We then assessed which positions and movements of the pitcher were isometric, concentric, eccentric, or any combination thereof. We learned that the pitcher's legs were primarily isometric; his shoulders and throwing forearm were both concentric and eccentric; the glove arm was isometric; and his low back and upper back were both isometric and concentric. In other words, traditional strength-training protocols, such as those that employ the Olympic lifts, to increase power, are not the best way to create and/or maintain velocity. In fact, the only true "power" movements of a pitcher are low back/upper back hyperextension into flexion and the throwing forearm moving from external rotation into internal rotation and ball launch.

It also became apparent that core/quad strength accounts for postural stability, especially head movement up or down. Surprisingly, our research shows that mandating a "tall" starting posture does not matter. In fact, the head will move down during left lift and stride forward to accommodate a pitcher's useable core/quad strength. In effect, the pitcher's body will find the specific height his core/quad strength can stabilize and sustain during his own unique delivery. This phenomenon is obviously subconscious and quite finely tuned. For example, in our research, we discovered that our pitchers assumed slightly different delivery postures when throwing the six-ounce, five-ounce, and four-ounce baseballs in our NPA over-and-under loading velocity study. They lowered their posture/center of gravity with the six-ounce ball and raised their posture/center of gravity with the four-ounce ball (compared to the baseline posture they established with the standard five-ounce ball).

With regard to the training regimens detailed in this section, it is important to note that:

- All of these training routines are cross specific to the rotational/directional biomechanics of an efficient delivery and designed to facilitate joint stability, total body flexibility, muscle endurance, muscle strength, cardiopulmonary stamina, and throwing arm speed.
- Whenever possible, training routines should be performed in three extremity positions (straight, supinate, pronate), three extremity movements (linear, circular, angular), and three torso planes (frontal, sagital, transverse).
- The recommended rotational training routines do not require machines and/or heavy free weights.
- All training protocols are implemented in some combination of closed-chain/open-chain work.
- Whenever possible, upper-body training progressions adhere to the following sequence: extremity position, scapular pinch, extremity pulse, extremity push, and extremity pull.
- All training protocols emphasize 80% rotational and 20% directional work ratios, with volume, load, frequency, intensity, and duration, to tolerance, in single sets with three-to-five reps per position and movement.

It should be noted that all of the experts who authored the chapters in this section (and their organizations) are part of and interact regularly with the NPA and its comprehensive network. Each of their chapters represents a "cliff note" contribution that identifies and explains selected exercise regimens that they utilize with their athletes to train function with rotational strength, endurance, and flexibility. The NPA and each of these contributors are committed to researching and developing safe, useable velocity protocols for the arm, bat, or club. It should be remembered at all times when these chapters are read that the traditional training paradigms have experienced a seismic shift as a result of better information and insight from medical science, exercise science, and coaching science.

5

National Pitching Association Rotational Conditioning Protocols for Real Velocity

(Tom Houses and Eric Barajas)

The NPA coaches have observed that the largest initial gains in velocity occur when a pitcher gets stronger with his useable strength. The following formula that looks at the workload done by a pitcher's upper body and arms can be used to calculate velocity/intensity:

<u>Anterior (accelerating) force X accelerating time "X"</u> =
three muscle groups

<u>Posterior (decelerating) force X accelerating time "X"/2</u>
two muscle groups

OR

fastballs are accelerated by
three muscle groups in "X" time
and
fastballs are decelerated by
two muscle groups in "X"/2 time

OR

posterior force (workloads) = 4/3 anterior force (workloads)
in half the time (twice the intensity)

The legs and core must have enough functional strength, endurance, and flexibility to stabilize posture, deliver an optimal total-body stride for maximum directional momentum, create 40°-60° of hip/shoulder separation and delay shoulder rotation, and keep the spine and torso upright, while the glove firms up in front of the torso over the landing foot and the throwing forearm lays back into external rotation. In that regard, the following formula can be used to calculate what must be done to functionally train the joint integrity elements (plastic stabilizers) and the muscles and connective tissue around the joint that is moving (elastic conduits) for energy recruitment. It shows, for example, that if a pitcher's mechanics are only 88% efficient, he needs to be 12% stronger to handle his competitive pitch totals.

$$\text{Joint integrity} = \frac{\text{physical conditioning x pitching workloads}}{\text{Biomechanical efficiency factor}}$$

Upper-body Training Volume/Week

For years, we've used the upper body formula to calculate a pitcher's throwing workload. All factors considered, it puts all the pieces together for a given week of training/pitching. One of its most meaningful features is the added strength loss variable (it's a given that over the course of a season, all pitchers lose arm strength). Keep in mind that training volumes/ratios should reflect 80% rotational momentum/20% directional momentum velocity contribution.

No. of game pitches/week x velocity^2 x .01 x $\dfrac{1}{\text{Biomechanical efficiency factor}}$ x $\dfrac{1}{\text{strength loss factor}}$ = ft-lbs of work while throwing a baseball

When developing upper body strength for real velocity, anything heavier than six ounces lifted fast with intensity probably won't help arm speed, mechanical efficiency, or joint health. The factor .01 is derived with a five-ounce ball as follows:

1/2 mass x velocity^2 = 1/2 5 oz. x 90 mph^2 = $\dfrac{1/2 \ (5/16 \text{lb})}{(32.2 \ \text{ft.})^2}$ x $\dfrac{(90 \ \text{mph}) \ \text{x} \ 5280 \ \text{ft/mile})^2}{3600 \ \text{sec/hr.}}$ = .014 ft/lb

At the NPA, we have learned by trial and error, a lot about how to train a pitcher to throw a fastball with real velocity. This chapter presents a typical workout from the NPA's 12-week SUV (Safe Useable Velocity) program. It should be noted that while a number of exercises could enhance each of the six variables that affect *Fastball Fitness*, only a representative sample is highlighted in this chapter.

The NPA's efforts to identify the most effective way to train pitchers to throw a fastball with real velocity have yielded a number of discoveries. For example, with regard to pitch totals/workloads, pitchers are only as strong as their weakest link. Furthermore, there must be parity in a pitcher's pre-game physical preparation, if performance parity is to exist in his competition and/or post-game recovery. The following "in-game" performance issues illustrate the importance of such parity:

- Significant change in fastball velocity = endurance/stamina problem
- Missing location right/left = posture = core/quad strength problem
- Missing location north/south = glove side = extremity strength problem

Post game issues, or "hot spots," in repair and recovery also can exist, for example:

- Frontside shoulder/elbow hot spots = mechanics
- Backside shoulder/elbow hot spots = strength imbalance between accelerator and decelerators:

  ✓ upper body:
  - three muscle groups accelerate in "x" time
  - two muscle groups decelerate in "x/2" time

  ✓ lower body:
  - four muscle groups accelerate
  - two muscle groups decelerate

The Titleist Performance Institute has conducted research that shows how important the flexibility/strength relationship is to a golfer's drive and a pitcher's fastball, for example:

- A hyperflexible 16-year-old golfer can drive the ball 300+ yards but can't stay in the fairway because while he has plenty of flexibility, he does not have enough strength to stabilize consistent contact with club and ball.
- The same golfer at age 36 can drive the ball accurately 300+ yards because he has flexibility *and* strength.
- The same golfer at 56 years old has the strength to drive the ball accurately, although not as far as two decades earlier, because he has lost flexibility.

If you replace the words "golfer/drive" with "pitcher/baseball," you get the picture. At the NPA, we've also learned that too much muscle without flexibility is just as bad as too little muscle with great flexibility. Furthermore, at the NPA, we've determined that while power lifting may be good for muscle, it is very hard on the body's joints and connective tissue. Accordingly, our power training is limited to throwing the four-, five-, and six-ounce velocity balls, and exercising on the back-extension machine using two-to-four pound exerballs.

At the NPA, we've also learned that monotonous overtraining (too much work, not enough recovery) causes neural stagnation and velocity declines. In this regard, a pitcher's best gains in velocity occur when he performs the recommended conditioning program routines three times per week, in addition to two sessions of skill work, all-the-while emphasizing active recovery. If a pitcher could not recover in at most two days, we found that we had to look differently at strength, endurance, and stamina issues involving that individual. In those situations, we had to focus more on repair aspects of his micro-cycles than prepare factors. The following two post-workout recovery issues illustrate the NPA's approach:

- Stiff and sore after 48 hours = more light endurance training work, less open-chain (heavy) resistance training
- "Dead arm" = more aerobic activity, more flat-ground throwing, less anaerobic activity, less mound throwing between training sessions

It should be noted that the workout routine detailed in the following sections only highlight and illustrate a few of the more recently developed NPA conditioning protocols. The same approach has been taken with chapters 6 through 9. Individuals who would like to obtain a more complete listing of the recommended training programs from each contributing author should go to each author's website, which is listed at the end of each chapter.

❑ Core-temperature elevation routine:
- Jog forward and backward
- Flex "T"s
- Carioca right and left
- Skip forward and backward

❑ Integrated flexibility routine:
- Hip rotations, with left and right feet together
- Hip rotations, with left and right feet shoulder-width apart
- Hip rotations, with left and right feet wider than shoulder-width apart
- Ankles—side/circles/figure 8
- Knees—side/circles/figure 8
- Shoulder pinches—up/forward/backward
- Shoulder circles—forward/backward
- Elbow pulls—palms in/up/down (Figure 5-1)
- Forearm crosses—palms in/up/down
- Forearms over and under—palms in/up/down
- Forearm pulls—side-to-side
- Forearm pulls—circles/forward/backward
- Forearm pulls—swim/forward/backward
- Anterior palm presses—three positions for one minute each (Figures 5-2 to 5-4)
- Posterior palm presses—one position for three minutes (Figure 5-5)

Figure 5-1

Figure 5-2

Figure 5-3

Figure 5-4

Figure 5-5

❑ Dynamic flexibility routine:
- Knee tucks
- Internal hip rotation
- Quad pull
- Lunge forward
- Lunge backward
- Stationary spider
- Inch worm
- Grasshopper
- Long-distance carioca right and left, with the arms down, the arms up (in flex "T")

Flex Work

❑ Back extension machine routine:
- Hyperextension, with hold (Figures 5-6 and 5-7)
- Hyperextension, with rotation and hold to both sides (Figures 5-8 to 5-11)
- Hyperextension, with rotation to both sides, with eccentric contraction
- Hands on ground, with hyperflexion; draw bellybutton to spine, e.g., mad cat (Figures 5-12 and 5-13)

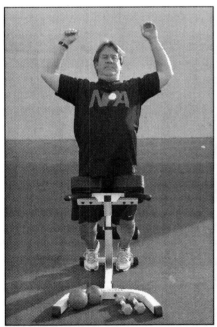

Figure 5-6

Figure 5-7

Figure 5-8

Figure 5-9

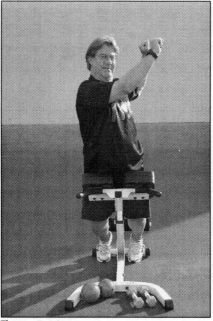
Figure 5-10

Figure 5-11

Figure 5-12

Figure 5-13

Plyoball/Dumbbell Work

❑ Long-distance carioca routine:
  • Arms down, with dumbbells
  • Arms up, in a flex "T," with dumbbells (Figures 5-14 to 5-16)

Figure 5-14

Figure 5-15

Figure 5-16

Figure 5-17

Figure 5-18

Figure 5-19

❑ Model walk (plyoball) routine:
  • With a four-pound exerball, walk forward with rotation; rotate to the side that the front foot hits (Figures 5-17 to 5-19).
  • With a four-pound exerball, walk backward with rotation; rotate to the side that the front foot hits.
❑ Lunge thrusts (plyoball) routine:
  • Lunge forward; rotate pelvis up; hyperextend back (Figures 5-20 and 5-21).
  • Lunge forward; rotate pelvis up; hyperextend back; squat (Figures 5-22 and 5-23).
  • Lunge forward; rotate pelvis up; hyperextend back; squat and rotate (Figure 5-24).

- ❑ Standing twist with partner (plyoball) routine:
  - Rotate through the hips; hand the ball to partner; keep hips stable (if no partner available, use wall).
- ❑ Standing twist wall toss (plyoball) routine:
  - Place feet roughly at a 45-degree angle; toss the plyoball from both sides (Figures 5-25 to 5-27).
  - Wall clocks (Figures 5-28 to 5-30)
  - Flex-T wall bounces (Figures 5-31 to 5-32)

Figure 5-20

Figure 5-21

Figure 5-22

Figure 5-23

Figure 5-24

Figure 5-25

Figure 5-26

Figure 5-27

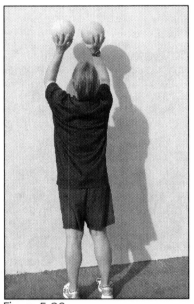

Figure 5-28

Figure 5-29

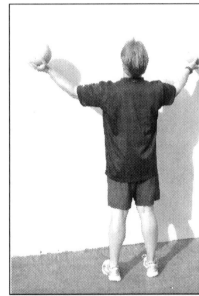

Figure 5-30

Figure 5-31

Figure 5-32

❏ Horizontal core (plyoball) routine:
- With the back at a 45-degree angle and the exerball between the knees, rotate the hips side-to-side.
- With the back at a 45-degree angle and the exerball between the knees, perform clock/counter clockwise circles.
- With the back at a 45-degree angle and the exerball between the knees, do a figure 8.
- With the shoulders off the ground and the exerball between the knees, rotate the hips side-to-side.
- With the shoulders off the ground and the exerball between the knees, do clock/counter clockwise circles.
- With the shoulders off the ground and the exerball between knees, do a figure 8.
- On the back and the exerball between the knees, rotate the hips side-to-side.
- On the back and the exerball between the knees, do clock/counter clockwise circles.
- On the back and the exerball between the knees, do a figure 8.
- On the back and the exerball between the knees and in the hands with the arms extended, do knees left, arms right, knees right, arms left (Figures 5-33 to 5-35).

Figure 5-33   Figure 5-34   Figure 5-35

❑ Back extension machine with dumbbells routine:
  • Hyperextension, with hold (Figures 5-36 and 5-37)
  • Hyperextension, with rotation and hold to both sides
  • Hyperextension, with rotation to both sides. with eccentric contraction (Figures 5-38 and 5-39)
  • Hyperextension, with rotation to both sides, with eccentric contraction and slow throwing motion

Figure 5-36

Figure 5-37

Figure 5-38

Figure 5-39

- ❑ Back-extension machine with plyoball routine:
  - Hyperextension, with hold
  - Hyperextension, with rotation and hold to both sides
  - Hyperextension, with rotation to both sides, with eccentric contraction
  - Hyperextension, with rotation to both sides, with eccentric contraction and throw (Figures 5-40 to 5-45)
- ❑ Standing critical-link (cords and grips) routine:
  - This routine entails the standard cord and grip exercise protocol involving 12 basic exercises that has been detailed in a number of previous NPA publications.
- ❑ Plyoball toss routine:
  - Horizontal
  - Two-knee hips/shoulders (perpendicular)
  - Two-knee hips/shoulders (angular)
  - Back-extension machine bounce-backs

Figure 5-40   Figure 5-41   Figure 5-42

Figure 5-43   Figure 5-44   Figure 5-45

Body Work

❑ Prone holds routine:
  • Elbows under shoulders; feet shoulder-width apart (Figure 5-46)
  • Elbows under shoulders; one foot up
  • One arm extended; feet shoulder-width apart
  • One arm extended; opposite foot in a foot-up position

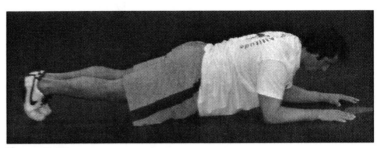

Figure 5-46

❑ Table tops routine:
  • With the hands under the armpits, and the feet under the knees at 90°, lift the butt/torso off the ground (Figure 5-47).
  • With the hands and the forearms on the ground, the elbows under the armpits, and the feet under the knees at 90°, lift the butt/torso off the ground (Figure 5-48).
  • With the hands on the chest, the elbows even with the armpits, and the feet under the knees at 90°, lift the butt/torso off the ground (Figure 5-49).

Figure 5-47

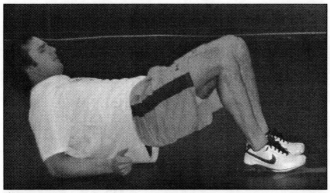
Figure 5-48

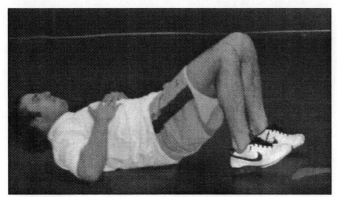
Figure 5-49

❏ Elbow holds routine:
   • With the hands at the hips, lift the upper body.
   • With the hands at the chest, lift the upper body.
   • With the hands under the armpits, lift the upper body.
   • With the hands behind the head, lift the upper body.
   • Repeat the first four exercises in the elbow-holds routine, but lift at the glutes.
   • Repeat the first four exercises in the elbow-holds routine, but lift at the heels.
❏ Flex "T" pushups (do not let the shoulders go below the elbows) routine:
   • Hands straight (Figures 5-50 to 5-52)
   • Hands facing each other (Figure 5-53)
   • Hands pointed out (Figure 5-54)
   • Hands straight, one foot up
   • Hands facing each other, one foot up
   • Hands pointed out, one foot up

Figure 5-50

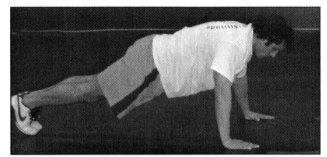

Figure 5-51

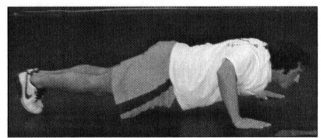

Figure 5-52

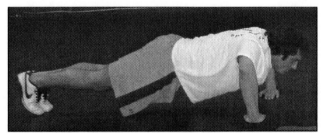

Figure 5-53

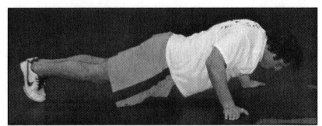

Figure 5-54

- ❏ Side-ups routine:
  - With the elbow under the shoulder, hold (Figure 5-55).
  - With the elbow under the shoulder, lift the hips up/down.
  - With the elbow under the shoulder, rotate the hips forward (Figure 5-56).
  - With the elbow under the shoulder, rotate the hips with short eccentric contractions.
  - With the elbow under the shoulder and the other hand on the floor, lift the hips up and down.
  - With the elbow under the shoulder and the other hand on the floor, rotate the hips.
  - With the elbow under the shoulder, hold, and lift the top foot up.
  - With the elbow under the shoulder, lift the hips up and down; lift the top foot up.
  - With the elbow under the shoulder, rotate the hips forward; lift the top foot up.
- ❏ Butt-ups (pinch the shoulder blades together) routine:
  - Hands by the hips straight out, and the legs straight
  - Hands by the hips facing each other, and the legs straight
  - Hands by the hips pointed out, and the legs straight
  - Hands by the hips straight out, and the legs crossed (Figure 5-57)
  - Hands by the hips facing each other, and the legs crossed
  - Hands by the hips pointing out, and the legs crossed

Figure 5-55

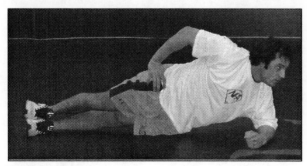

Figure 5-56

Figure 5-57

❑ Low-back routine:
  • Superman, hold.
  • Alternating superman, lift the opposite arm and leg.
  • Same side superman, lift the same arm and leg.
  • On the hands and knees, extend the opposite arm and leg, and hold.
  • On the hands and knees, extend the opposite arm and leg, and repeat.
  • On the hands and knees, extend the opposite arm and leg with toes up, and hold.
  • On the hands and knees, extend the opposite arm and leg with toes up, and repeat.
❑ Wall-work end-range training routine:
  • Isometric arm work:
      ✓ anterior (Figures 5-58 to 5-60)
      ✓ posterior (Figures 5-61 to 5-63)

Figure 5-58

Figure 5-59

The aforementioned routines represent a somewhat abbreviated version of the NPA's rotational conditioning program. As was noted in a previous chapter, the statistical summary of the NPA's most recent velocity study validates the necessity of a paradigm shift concerning how pitchers should be trained to pitch a baseball. The results of this study also help reinforce the validity of what the other "experts" are doing around the sports world to train their throwers/strikers. In that regard, the efforts and findings of four of the most respected sport scientists and organizations in the world are detailed in Chapters 6 through 9.

Figure 5-60

Figure 5-61

Figure 5-62

Figure 5-63

6

Titleist Performance Institute Conditioning Protocols for Real Velocity

(Greg Rose)

One of the key principles in the golf world that directly correlates into creating a faster pitch in the baseball world is that in order to increase your body's speed of rotation, you must first develop the ability to support and stabilize rotation. In other words, if you train to increase your body's ability to rotate and deliver speed, but your core and base of support can't handle the increased loads or speed, then your training will not produce the desired results. The following series of exercises involves the four drills that we utilize at the Titleist Performance Institute to help stabilize rotation.

Diagonal-Chops, Stable-Base Exercise Series

The diagonal-chops, stable-base series is designed to teach the body how to stabilize the large speeds and forces that are produced in the arms. The key to maximizing the benefits of performing the exercises in this series is to avoid moving your torso and lower body. Your arms should only be allowed to move diagonally across the front of your body, while trying to keep your trunk and hips facing forward at all times. The exercise series entails four leg positions—each increasing in difficulty of stabilization as the exercise progresses. All of the leg positions mimic the release stance when pitching a baseball.

❑ Half-kneeling chop drill: (Figures 6-1 to 6-3):

A cable-cross machine and a bar attachment (a tricep rope can be an alternative to the bar) are required to perform this exercise. To do the drill, assume a half kneeling position, with your down knee away from the machine or the door. Next, grab the bar with both hands on top of the bar, while keeping your posture as tall as possible. Perform a chop diagonally across your body, keeping your hands and the bar close to your chest throughout the movement. Don't allow your shoulders to rotate. Slowly return to the starting position. Repeat the appropriate number of sets and reps.

Figure 6-1

Figure 6-2

Figure 6-3

❑ Lunge-stance chop drill: (Figures 6-4 to 6-6):
This drill is performed in a standing position in order to get into a more functional baseball-delivery position. A cable-cross machine with a bar attachment (a tricep rope can be an alternative to the bar) is required to do the exercise. To perform the exercise, get into a lunge stance, with your front knee positioned closest to the machine. Set the pulley to the highest position and grab the bar with both hands on top of the bar, while keeping your posture as tall as possible. Then, perform a chop diagonally down and across your body, keeping your hands and the bar close to your chest throughout the movement. Don't allow your shoulders to rotate with each chop. Focus on keeping your torso stable. Just move your arms and shoulders.

Figure 6-4

Figure 6-5

Figure 6-6

❑ Single-leg chop drill: (Figures 6-7 to 6-9):
This drill incorporates the instability of a Swiss ball for the lower body and is designed to really challenge your lower body and core. A cable-cross machine with a bar attachment (a tricep rope can be an alternative to the bar) is required to do the exercise. To perform the exercise, assume a lunge stance, with your front knee positioned closest to the machine and your back leg placed on top of a Swiss ball. Set the pulley to the highest position, and grab the bar with both hands on top of the bar, while keeping your posture as tall as possible. Then, perform a chop diagonally down and across your body, keeping your hands and the bar close to your chest throughout the movement. Don't allow your shoulders or lower body to rotate with each chop. Focus on keeping your torso stable. Just move your arms and shoulders.

Figure 6-7

Figure 6-8

Figure 6-9

❑ Single-leg, unstable-base chop drill (Figures 6-10 to 6-12):
This drill offers the ultimate challenge in lower-body stability. As such, it should be performed with extreme care. A cable-cross machine with a bar attachment (a tricep rope can be an alternative to the bar) are required to do the exercise. To perform the exercise, assume a lunge stance, with your front knee positioned closest to the machine, your front foot on an Airex pad (to create more instability), and your back leg placed on top of a Swiss ball. Set the pulley to the highest position, and grab the bar with both hands on top of the bar, while keeping your posture as tall as possible. Then, perform a chop diagonally down and across your body, keeping your hands and the bar close to your chest throughout the movement. Don't allow your shoulders or lower body to rotate with each chop. Focus on keeping your torso stable. Just move your arms and shoulders.

Figure 6-10

Figure 6-11

Figure 6-12

A Call for Action

Adding the four aforementioned diagonal "chops" exercises to your training regimen can develop your body's ability to support and stabilize rotation. Similar to how they help a golfer achieve greater distance on his drives, these exercises can enhance a pitcher's ability to throw a fastball with real velocity. Additional information on the conditioning programs and programs employed at Titleist Performance Institute can be obtained by visiting our website at www.mytpi.com.

7

Elite Baseball Academy Conditioning Procols for Real Velocity

(Mike Paul)

In a day and age where the ability of an athlete to pitch is often overshadowed by what the speed gun reads, it is obvious that coaches must adjust their thinking. Much of the information presented in this chapter is based upon the results of a study that we conducted recently at the Elite Baseball Academy—an effort that was undertaken out of necessity. As a personal pitching coach and professional scout with the Minnesota Twins, I see many young arms go by the wayside. I know they are mechanically sound, but they lack the velocity to pitch at the next level.

The conditioning protocols and program detailed in this book are designed to be the difference-maker for those pitchers who want to enhance their ability to throw with real velocity. The key is that the athlete must do the recommended work. The protocols involved in this study have created significant velocity improvements in those athletes who have consistently expended the time and energy to perform the recommended training regimen.

While almost no one is foolish enough to believe that every pitcher can develop the ability to throw a 90-mph fastball, it's very frustrating for me to look back in my career and think of all the athletes I've trained who threw 84-86 mph, whom I could not help throw harder. In that regard, the information, instruction, and insights offered in *Fastball Fitness* could have helped me then and will assist anyone who seriously considers it in the future.

At the Elite Baseball Academy, our velocity-training regimen is referred to as Elite T.M.T. (torque—momentum—timing). The throwing portion of the program basically consists of the traditional, glorified crow hop. The only difference is that the athlete does the work at 120 feet, while maintaining balance and posture, stride and momentum, and a solid opposite-and-equal-into-foot strike. In other words, he incorporates perfect pitching mechanics, while performing the throwing routine.

The recommended training progression involves several elements. After properly warming up, the athlete performs T.M.T. with maximum intensity at 120 feet, throwing the ball eight times. He then allows his body to cool down. Next, he repeats the process two times. Our research enabled us to discover that if the athlete's body is strengthened with the proper training protocols for optimizing stress, stride, and momentum, his body will *self time*, and maximum velocity will be achieved. Table 7-1 illustrates the extent of positive velocity improvements that we have been able to achieve as a result of our training at the Elite Baseball Academy.

Age	Velocity Week 1	Velocity Week 5	Velocity Week 8	Added Velocity
13-yr-old	79	81	81	2 mph
14-yr-old	68	70	70	2 mph
15-yr-old	64	67	70	6 mph
16-yr-old	73	78	80	7 mph
16-yr-old	79	82	82	3 mph
16-yr-old	74	79	80	6 mph
17-yr-old	83	86	88	5 mph
17-yr-old	83	87	90	7 mph
18-yr-old	84	86	88	4 mph
18-yr-old	84	89	89	5 mph
18-yr-old	79	82	85	6 mph
20-yr-old	84	87	88	4 mph
21-yr-old	79	80	83	4 mph
27-yr-old	89	92	94	5 mph

Table 7-1. Velocity chart

Cross-Specific Body Work

At the Elite Baseball Academy, we require pitchers to perform T.M.T. training twice a week and the following workout three times a week (note: all exercises are executed on both sides):

- Vertical warm-up
- Running drills
- Knee drills
- Step-behinds

- T.M.T.
- Pull-up routine (Figures 7-1 to 7-8)
- Dips
- Six-position lunges (Figures 7-9 to 7-14)
- Push-ups
- Clock drills
- Tubing
- Six-position medicine-ball work (Figures 7-15 to 7-25)
- Cool down/jog

It's important to keep in mind that the significant velocity increases that the participants in our study achieved were accomplished with functional strength, endurance, and flexibility training alone. No weighted-baseball work was involved. Much of the training in the study was undertaken as part of our normal routine. The primary deviation from our regular program was involved performing T.M.T. and the pull-up routine. Our observations of what actions are involved when a pitcher's arm works led us to include eccentric, concentric, and isometric movements in the workouts for pitchers. As Table 7-1 indicates, the results were impressive.

When considering the increases in velocity that the participants in our study achieved, it is important to remember that velocity is only one facet of pitching. The athlete must also have the ability to locate the ball, change speeds, and remain healthy. All other factors considered, however, velocity appears to be the major quantitative factor that creates "opportunity" for pitchers. Accordingly, the thinking of coaches who want to enhance the ability of their pitchers to throw with real velocity must evolve.

Figure 7-1

Figure 7-2

Figure 7-3

Figure 7-4

Figure 7-5

Figure 7-6

Figure 7-7

Figure 7-8

Figure 7-9

Figure 7-10

Figure 7-11

Figure 7-12

Figure 7-13

Figure 7-14

Figure 7-15

Figure 7-16

Figure 7-17

Figure 7-18

Figure 7-19

Figure 7-20

Figure 7-21

Figure 7-22

Figure 7-23

Figure 7-24

Figure 7-25

8

Beacon Orthopedics/ Champion Sports Conditioning Protocols for Real Velocity

(Troy Merckle)

When determining the most effective dynamic flexibility and strength exercises to be included in a particular conditioning regimen, strong consideration should be given to the neuromuscular and proprioceptive demands of the activity for which the exercises are being selected. As such, "waking up as many neuromuscular phone lines" as possible should be the primary objective of any preparatory activity.

Rotational Stretching and Strengthening

Increased flexibility can be defined as elongation of soft tissue. The main purpose of improving tissue length is to allow the targeted area being able to respond with less micro-trauma when placed in a position during a specified activity. Increased pliability also enables the soft tissue to potentially contribute more towards the activity, increasing the possibility of enhancing performance. Considerable research has been undertaken to determine the safest, most effective form of stretching, whether it be static, ballistic, PNF approaches, etc. In fact, the findings of these investigative efforts have been subjected to substantial myopic interpretation by some coaches and medical clinicians. For example, concern exists in some circles that incorporating rotational stretching and strengthening in an athlete's conditioning regimen may place undue stress on his lumbar spine.

The primary point to keep in mind, however, is that the main focus of any preparatory activity should be that of getting the body ready to perform the "motions" of the activity involved. In this regard, although isolated, joint-specific exercises may, at times, appear to be the appropriate option, a multi-joint, integrated approach should be strongly considered.

Perhaps, the most difficult issue to deal with concerning flexibility involves the problem that arises when flexibility is taken from the "stretching table" to the field. More often than not, the body is saying, "thanks for the increased flexibility, but what am I supposed to do with it?" The concept of dynamic flexibility attempts to address that issue.

Traditionally, the recommended stretching progression involves a routine of exercises that go from a slower, controlled environment to a higher-intensity, less-controlled environment. It should be noted that any "stretching" exercise should be performed after the core body temperature has been raised adequately in order to achieve increased pliability with the involved tissues. In that regard, dynamic strength exercises that incorporate a multi-planar approach are not only an efficient way to achieve that objective, they also help prepare the athlete for any of the required movements associated with his sport.

Suggested Training Protocol

The protocol that we employ at Beacon Orthopedics/Champion Sports for warming up and for developing dynamic flexibility can also be utilized for strengthening as well. Four variable factors determine the focus of the training regimen: load used, work-rest ratio, volume performed, and frequency of performing as it relates to a periodized approach. It should be noted that the recommended exercises target the entire closed kinematic chain, beginning at the foot and working up through the cervical spine. Furthermore, each of the exercises involves several phases that collectively address all three planes of motion. In order for rotational force (the transverse plane) to be developed maximally, the frontal and sagital plane motion segments need to be free from restrictions as well.

The recommended training program for developing dynamic rotational flexibility, as well as strength, entails three primary types of exercises: step-ups, reaches, and lunges with punches. Each of the exercises within a particular classification can be used for stretching and strengthening and incorporate a multi-planar approach.

STEP-UPS

❑ Forward step-up:
- Center of mass is shifted over the foot on the box, which forces him to use linear energy to perform the required task (Figures 8-1 and 8-2).
- To develop flexibility, start at the ground and note the increased stretching of the gastroc/soleus complex.
- Core stability is noted throughout the entire lift in order to allow a smooth, efficient motion.
- Balance point is achieved at the top of the movement (Figure 8-3).

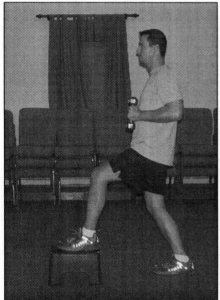
Figure 8-1

Figure 8-2

Figure 8-3

❑ Cross-over step-up (Figures 8-4 and 8-5):
  • This exercise is an effective stretch/strengthening move for the hip external rotators and abductors, especially during the "down" part of the movement.

Figure 8-4

Figure 8-5

❑ Rotational step-up (Figures 8-6 to 8-8):
  • The beginning movement involves having the feet positioned perpendicular to each other.
  • The athlete shifts his center of mass over his lead leg before initiating the up move.

Figure 8-6

Figure 8-7

Figure 8-8

REACHES

❑ Forward reach:
  • The hands are raised above the head, i.e., the arms are glued to the ears (Figure 8-9).
  • The knee is slightly flexed, but remains fixed throughout the movement, i.e., the foot that is on the ground.
  • The opposite leg should be driven back for counter balance (Figures 8-10 and 8-11, side view).

Figure 8-9

Figure 8-10

Figure 8-11

❑ Left reach:
  • The right arm is above the head and glued to the ear (Figure 8-12).
  • If on the right leg, this move targets scapular loading and unloading, as well as concentric and eccentric hip adductor control (Figure 8-13).

Figure 8-12

Figure 8-13

❑ Right reach:
 • The left arm is above the head and glued to the ear (Figure 8-14).
 • If on the right leg, this move targets hip/lumbar rotation that is closely related to follow-through (Figure 8-15).

Figure 8-14

Figure 8-15

LUNGES WITH PUNCHES

❏ Forward (starting position—Figure 8-16):
  • Low punches—right and left (Figures 8-17 and 8-18)
  • Medium punches—right and left (Figures 8-19 and 8-20)
  • High punches—right and left (Figures 8-21 and 8-22)

Figure 8-16

Figure 8-17

Figure 8-18

Figure 8-19

Figure 8-20

Figure 8-21   Figure 8-22

❑ Lateral (starting position—Figure 8-23):
  • Low punches—right and left (Figures 8-24 and 8-25)
  • Medium punches—right and left (Figures 8-26 and 8-27)
  • High punches—right and left (Figures 8-28 and 8-29)

Figure 8-23   Figure 8-24   Figure 8-25

Figure 8-26

Figure 8-27

Figure 8-28

Figure 8-29

❑ Rotational: (starting position—Figure 8-30):
- Low punches—right and left (Figures 8-31 and 8-32)
- Medium punches—right and left (Figures 8-33 and 8-34)
- High punches—right and left (Figures 8-35 and 8-36)

Figure 8-30

Figure 8-31

Figure 8-32

Figure 8-33

Figure 8-34

Figure 8-35

Figure 8-36

9

Victorian Institute of Sports Conditioning Protocols for Real Velocity

(Simon Webb)

This chapter is designed to provide pitchers with a practical training program that specifically trains and prepares the body for rotation, using innovative flexibility and resistance exercises. Increasing the body's ability to produce force in rotation, while simultaneously decreasing muscle imbalance, allows the pitcher to repeatedly apply maximum force through his kinetic chain and reduce the likelihood of injury. This chapter provides every pitcher something new to work on in the gym. Those individuals who have been doing the same old strength-training routine in the weight room will find a new stretch or a new resistance exercise to give their conditioning regime a kick start.

The physiological model of training elite athletes who want to enhance their athletic performance has been largely contradictory in nature. Exercise training programs have typically been designed to improve strength bilaterally and in isolation, with most athletes still stretching individual muscles statically as part of their warm up. The majority of the strength and flexibility exercises in such regimens are closed-chain activities that are done in the gym, with little gain or transfer onto the sporting arena. If the paradigm of training elite athletes and the shift that is required in their exercise programs versus the paradox of what is currently being done are examined, it can be seen that very few athletes train to improve the symmetry of their strength and range of movement or improve their kinetic chain.

As a conditioning coach for elite athletes, every book that I have ever read about improving strength for a sport or skill always seems to be missing something. The suggested gym exercises are almost always the same; the only thing that is different is the person performing the exercise. It is always about increasing strength for the pecs, lats, delts, and legs. Recently, the trend has focused on improving core stability.

Again, everything I read makes me ask the question, "How are these exercises relevant to developing strength and power for pitching?" They all involve applying force bilaterally, usually through a single muscle, joint, or plane of movement. Unfortunately, they have overlooked the fundamental movement that occurs in all sporting situations—rotation. Not only have they not incorporated this factor into their recommended training programs, they have overlooked what should be the key focus of any athletic training program—the ability to transfer any strength gains made in the gym onto the mound. They fail to realize that training the body in rotation enhances a pitcher's ability to improve his kinematic sequence and ensure optimal movement efficiency when he's pitching.

During the over ten years that I have been training elite athletes, I have seen many trainers try and incorporate the aforementioned exercises in their conditioning regimens. In fact, many of the so-called traditional, which can be found in every gym around the world, are entrenched in training programs, regardless of the sport or activity for which the athlete trains. These exercises, such as the bench press, squats, shoulder press, and lat pulldowns, are all widely accepted for improving general strength and power. The primary problem with having pitchers perform these traditional exercises is that while the body does get stronger, it only does so in that movement and in isolation to the rest of the body. Furthermore, the strength that is developed has no practical application. When it comes to pitching (and all other sporting situations for that matter), a single muscle never works in isolation and independently from the rest of the body. As a result, coaches and trainers are faced with a dilemma concerning how to transfer any strength gained in the gym into power on the mound when pitching.

Contemporary trends concerning rotation training have focused on 'core stability' and more recently 'functional-strength' training. This approach attempts to improve the strength of the musculature of the spine and abdomen. True rotational training, however, doesn't just isolate the abdominal wall or train the body in a single plane of movement. It specifically targets the anterior shoulder girdle, along with abdominal support and the contralateral (opposite) hip flexor/quadriceps. Although some trainers have adopted this concept and strategy to improve strength and the body's kinetic chain, this approach only involves doing half the job. The posterior muscles must also be trained to work in a coordinated way to assist in achieving greater power output. The muscles that must work posteriorly with a simultaneous contraction are the latissimus dorsi via the thoracolumbar fascia to the opposite gluteus maximus. The contralateral anterior and posterior muscles work in a coordinated, sequential order to create optimal spinal rotation and produce maximal efficiency and power. As Figure 9-1 illustrates, the muscles (both anteriorly and posteriorly) interact in a contralateral and sequential fashion to develop spinal rotation.

Figure 9-1

The aforementioned factor has significance for the pitcher who is trying to improve his rotational strength in the gym. For example, a right-handed pitcher must train a cross pattern to develop and transfer energy into the baseball that involves his right pectoralis and shoulder girdle with his left oblique muscles and left hip flexor/quad. At the same time, the left latissimus dorsi and right gluteus maximus must also be trained to produce in order force to create efficient rotation of the spine.

The gross movement in a cross pattern that should occur every time the body applies force around the spine has been identified by kinesiologists, biomechanists, and physical therapists. It is this pattern that many strength and conditioning specialists have failed to incorporate into their recommended training programs. Adhering to such a pattern can help enhance the specificity of weight training and facilitate the transfer of any strength and power gains achieved in the gym into improved athletic performance, while decreasing the athlete's potential for injury.

As Figure 9-2 illustrates, a neutral spine allows for greater rotational torque, similar to a spinning top, than a spine that is not in correct alignment and has compromised movement. This image shows how force can be lost and why improving efficiency is important when training spinal rotation.

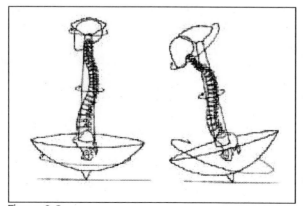

Figure 9-2

The question arises concerning why training this specific cross pattern is so important in assisting not only strength development but also injury prevention. The answer is straightforward. The spine acts as the structural foundation to all movement, as force is either transferred through or around the spine. To maximize energy transfer, the spine requires structural integrity (alignment) and a stable base (pelvis) from which to operate. Pitchers have a very high volume of a repetitive movement pattern. By always using the same muscles to develop power, those muscles become stronger and tighter than other muscles in the body. This situation leads to muscle imbalances and spinal malalignment, specifically related to the highly specialized and repetitive movements in which pitchers engage.

Dominant muscles further contribute to muscle imbalance. Because they tend to inhibit weaker antagonist muscles, these weaker muscles then suffer from de-conditioning, which often makes it impossible to teach or correct motor patterns. All of these problems are usually followed by pain and, eventually, by permanent structural dysfunction. As such, improved flexibility of the spine aids in postural alignment and subsequently strength development and injury prevention.

The importance of quality movement and an understanding how it is lost have dramatically challenged the traditional approaches to training athletes to compete. It has been a very common practice with developmental athletes to spend the major portion of the early work in their training developing their technique, with little or no regard for strength and conditioning. In fact, the number of hours a pitcher spends practicing the highly specialized and repetitive nature of the pitching technique in isolation will have a negative impact biomechanically on muscle function and will increase his potential for being injured and for incurring postural problems.

As a conditioning specialist who works with throwers/pitchers, I often see many coaches who are trying to improve the pitching mechanics of their players by giving them specific instructions that focus on improving their technique. Over time, by continually executing the same motor pattern and trying to produce force to one side of the body, muscle imbalances will begin to occur. These imbalances will slowly decrease both movement efficiency and the body's ability to produce force, which eventually can lead to injury.

All factors considered, a pitcher's body will always try and find the path of least resistance when executing a skill. As such, every pitcher has his own unique signature or style of pitching, given that each person has a different level of muscle tightness and weakness throughout his body. It is important to keep in mind that sometimes the technique a coach advocates for an athlete wants may not be physically possible for the pitcher to achieve until he improves his body first.

Correct postural alignment is crucial to improving a pitcher's rotation and performance, and can be best described by using the analogy of a racing car.

A new car requires very little work to maintain its quality of function, very similar to that of a child. However, a racing car during a race is continually performing at or near maximum (revolutions), similar to a pitcher when he's in competition. Throughout the course of a race, a slight imbalance in the racing car's wheel alignment will have dramatic consequences for the car's overall performance. The tires begin to wear unevenly, thereby compromising the car's steering. Eventually, it becomes increasingly difficult to maintain accurate control of the vehicle. While all of these problems progressively get worse throughout the race, fuel economy is reduced, and overall performance is decreased. All of these other signs of wear can then lead to the vehicle eventually breaking down, but in other parts of the car, rather than the initial cause—the imbalance in wheel alignment.

A pitcher who neglects his muscular imbalances and postural misalignment will eventually experience the same breakdown process as the racing car. As a consequence, he will be required to work a lot harder to maintain the proper technical execution and to produce greater power output. Simultaneously, however, his potential for breakdown becomes a lot higher. Repair and restoration of the car's efficiency requires a lot of work, not too dissimilar to an athlete who is in rehabilitation.

Flexibility

To prepare the body for rotation, the first and most important step for improvement is to decrease muscle tightness, allow the weaker muscles to function properly, and increase range of movement. This goal is best achieved through a sound flexibility program. This step alone, even before starting a strength program, will help improve pitching mechanics and allow for greater kinetic transfer onto the baseball. Over the years, very few new stretches have been put forth, because—as was stated previously—almost everyone uses the same set of stretches for each muscle, regardless of the exercise's specificity to the overall action or to the athlete's individual needs.

Due to the elastic properties of muscle fibres, when muscle length is shortened for extended periods of time or when a muscle is very tight, it begins to pull on the bones to which it is attached. If the opposing muscle (antagonist) is weaker than its protagonist, it will then lengthen since it cannot overcome the pulling force to which it is being subjected. Subsequently, the position of the joint that is by this muscle may be affected. It is important to note that even though a muscle can be weak and somewhat lengthened, it can still have limited range of movement, and therefore also be considered tight. This factor is why an athlete should always stretch both sides of his body. In fact, he should stretch those areas of his body that are tight for at least twice as long as those muscles that are relatively flexible.

The following stretches target specific groups of muscles that have a direct impact on the spine and pelvis and, in turn, assist in developing strength in rotation. It should be noted that the flexibility exercises that are included in this section are not static stretches. Rather, they are very dynamic, more advanced, and require functional strength to have the stability that is needed to perform the movement. One of the major benefits of their inclusion is the fact that while stretching one muscle group, another or opposite muscle group must apply force to hold the position.

You should start with two sets of 30 seconds each and slowly build up to one minute. Remember that a pitcher is prone to developing muscular imbalances where one side of his body is tighter than the other. To overcome this situation, you must spend at least twice as long on the tight muscle in order to restore balance.

DISCLAIMER: Do not attempt any of these stretches or the following exercises if you suffer from an existing injury in the muscle or joint involved in the activity. If any of the following exercises causes discomfort or pain or if you are unsure of exactly how to perform any of the exercises, you should consult your local health/fitness professional.

Dynamic Stretches

❑ Prone glute—cross-pattern specific (Figures 9-3 and 9-4):
To perform the exercise, place a foam roller under one thigh and bend the knee to 90°. With both hands resting on the floor, extend the other leg back. Keep the pelvis square. Hold for five deep breaths. Then, take the opposite forearm in front of the bent leg and rest the elbow and hand on the floor. Apply force onto the arm and as you do, allow the shoulders to rotate and extend the other hand up to the sky. Try and keep the shoulders even.

Figure 9-3

Figure 9-4

❏ Shoulder rotation (Figure 9-5 and 9-6):
To perform the exercise, start on all fours next to a pole, with the hands shoulder-width apart. You should be at least an arm's length from the pole in this position. Make sure your armpit is in line with the pole. Take the hand that is furthest from the pole, slide it under the body, and grab the pole. Then, allow your chest to rotate towards the pole and allow the shoulder of the arm crossing your body to lower to the floor.

Figure 9-5

Figure 9-6

❑ Latissimus dorsi—Smith machine hang (Figures 9-7 and 9-8):
To perform the exercise, start by placing the bar at shoulder height. Then, stand sideways to the bar and grab it with one hand. Take a small step forward with the opposite foot and place your body weight on that leg. Slightly bend the knee and lift the other leg up and slide it as far from the pole as you can. Then, lower your pelvis diagonally to the floor. If you are not strong enough to support your body with one arm, use both hands to hold onto the bar.

Figure 9-7

Figure 9-8

❑ Kneeling hip flexor (Figure 9-9):
This exercise is the first part of a two-stretch progression. If you can perform this static stretch and control the posterior tilt of your pelvis, then you should progress to the overhead hip-flexor exercise.

Figure 9-9

❑ Overhead hip flexor (Figures 9-10 and 9-11):
To perform this exercise, start in a lunge position, about one foot from a pole. Make sure your back knee, pelvis, and shoulders are all in a vertical alignment with the posterior tilt of your pelvis so that the abs and the glutes of the back leg are engaged. Take the arm closest to the pole and hold on to the pole, with your elbow at the same height as your shoulder. Then, take the other arm up over your head, grabbing the pole slightly above head height. Maintaining the posterior tilt of the pelvis, lower your back knee to the floor by two inches and hold for 10 seconds. Then, lower your back leg, again by two inches. You should feel the stretch on the back leg at the top of the thigh.

Figure 9-10

Figure 9-11

Resistance Training

This section is specifically designed to provide throwers and pitchers with a practical training program that will enable them to develop strength in rotation and apply those strength gains from the exercise area onto the field and mound.

Increasing the flexibility and range of movement of a muscle or joint is only the first step when preparing the body for rotation. The next phase is to begin increasing the strength of the weaker antagonist muscles. Think about a game of tug-o-war with two competing 10-made teams—one made up of jockeys and the other of bodybuilders. Of course, the team of bodybuilders would win every time. To make the game more even would not be a matter of increasing the number of jockeys or decreasing the number of bodybuilders, but rather splitting the teams into five jockeys and five bodybuilders per side. Such an approach would create a much more even contest.

Similarly, when you are trying to restore muscle balance, your first step should not be just to improve the strength of the weaker muscle or simply increasing flexibility. Rather, to restore muscle balance in a manner that is more likely to result in permanent change, a more holistic approach that combines both a decrease in muscle tightness and an increase in the strength of the weaker muscle is required.

As was discussed previously, traditional gym exercises (especially those involving machines and cables) train the body by isolating a single muscle, joint, or plane of movement. The primary limitation with having a pitcher train with those traditional exercises is that while a pitcher's muscles and body may get stronger, it only does so in that movement.

Rotational training is different from normal strength training in a gym. In rotational training, you must be able to do basic exercises with a minimal load before your ego is otherwise allowed to intrude in the process. Keep in mind that unless the full chain and sequence along your spine is strengthened first, then your muscle recruitment will break down at its weakest point, and maximal energy transfer will be decreased.

A good place to start a rotational training program is by doing some functional exercises. The term "functional training" refers to performing gym or movement-based exercises that employ the specific muscles and movements that are utilized in sport performance. Functional training can help create a solid base for the body to apply force. Rotational training then involves doing a progression of functional exercises, while specifically incorporating and developing spinal rotation in the training regimen and targeting the cross patterns within the body in a sequential and coordinated manner. Progressing from performing functional exercises to also doing exercises that develop rotation should only occur when the pitcher has sound exercise technique. Failure to do so means that the likelihood of effective rotation is decreased, and the body will lose both efficiency and power.

Exercises for Developing Balance (Pelvic Stability)

The exercises that are included in this section are designed to give each pitcher, beginner through elite, a starting point. In each instance, a functional exercise is listed, followed by a progression of the same exercise that then incorporates rotation. Remember to start with the functional exercises first and only progress to the rotational exercises when you can perform them, using the proper technique.

❑ Wobble board (Figure 9-12):
To perform this exercise, start by standing on a wobble board with two feet. Then, lift one leg up to hip height and across your body to mimic the initial movement of pitching. Do not change your hip, spine, or shoulder alignment. Then, if you can maintain good balance, take the opposite hand out to the side and practice throwing a tennis ball. Do this on both sides of the body.

Figure 9-12

❑ Wobble board foot-plant start position (Figure 9-13):
This exercise is similar to the previous exercise, except for the fact that you start the exercise standing on a step or a plyo box. Then, step out onto the wobble board to help ensure stability of the pelvis upon your foot plant.

Figure 9-13

❑ Finish position (Figure 9-14):
To help enhance good balance technique, ensure that your front ankle, knee, and hip are all in alignment. To progress this exercise further, throw a tennis ball.

Figure 9-14

❑ Swiss ball bridge with knee extension—*functional* (Figure 9-15):
To perform the exercise, start with your shoulders on a Swiss ball and your ankles under your knees. Keep your pelvis in line with your shoulders and knees. Then, bring one foot off the ground so that the leg is now in a straight line. Do not drop either your pelvis or the hip of the leg being extended. Finally, do not excessively arch your lower back. Keep the leg extended.

Figure 9-15

❑ Swiss ball bridge with rotation—*rotation* (Figure 9-16):
To perform the exercise, start with your shoulders on the ball, with your ankles shoulder-width apart, and under your knees. Then, take a 2.5kg plate in your hands above your chest. Use the posterior muscles of the shoulder and spine to rotate on the ball in order to allow the hands to move across and to the side. Rotate and move your arms at the same speed as your shoulders. The plate should stay in line with the sternum throughout the movement. Try to not drop or initiate the movement with the hips.

Figure 9-16

❑ Swiss ball bridge with a medicine ball throw with rotation—*rotation* (Figure 9-17):

To perform the exercise, begin in the bridge position, with either a light medicine ball or a tennis ball. Both hands should be out to the side in the flexed-T position. Pull the scapulae against the Swiss ball and bring the hand to the chest to increase shoulder rotation. As your spine rotates, throw the medicine ball to a partner or wall.

Figure 9-17

❑ Single-arm seated row—*functional* (Figures 9-18 and 9-19):

This movement is similar to a standard seated row, except that, in this exercise, change the handle to a single-cable handle and use only one hand. Start the movement by allowing the shoulders and hand to rotate towards the weight stack. Then, initiate the pulling action with the scapulae and allow the spine to fully rotate, as the hand finishes near the ribs and chest.

Figure 9-18

Figure 9-19

❏ Smith machine pull and rotate—*rotation/start* (Figure 9-20):
The bar of the machine should be at a height so that when you are under the bar, your spine is parallel to the floor. Your knees should be above your ankles, and your hand should be above your chest. Similar to the previous exercise, the movement is initiated by pulling the scapulae to allow the spine to then rotate.

Figure 9-20

❏ Smith machine pull and rotate—*rotation/end* (Figure 9-21):
As the spine rotates and your shoulder moves closer to the bar, allow the elbow of the pulling arm to bend slightly. Try and keep the pelvis up and in line with your shoulders and knee. Do not allow either your pelvis to drop or your lower back to excessively arch.

Figure 9-21

❏ Smith machine pull and rotate—*rotation/advanced* (Figure 9-22):
More advanced, this exercise works the posterior cross pattern. Try not to lift or bend the leg that is extended as you pull and rotate your shoulders towards the bar.

Figure 9-22

❏ Back extension and rotation—*functional* (Figure 9-23):
To perform this exercise, position your feet against a wall and place your hips and thighs against a Swiss ball. Put one hand behind your ear (not on your head or neck) and the other on your hip, in order to avoid using your chest to gain any extra movement. Then, lower your chin and chest onto the ball. Slowly lift your head, shoulders, scapula, and spine up and then rotate to the side with your hand behind your ear. Feel your shoulder moving back to the wall, not the opposite chest moving forward. You should not feel pain or discomfort when performing this exercise, especially in your lower back.

Figure 9-23

❑ Back extension with a medicine ball throw on a mini tramp—*rotation* (Figure 9-24):

This exercise requires a back-extension machine (also sometimes referred to as a Roman chair), a mini tramp, and a light medicine ball. In order to perform this exercise, lower your chest down to the floor. As you come up, lift your head and shoulders first, not your lower back. As you come up even higher, turn and rotate your arm away from the mini tramp and set yourself in a flex-T position. Then, with minimal time at the top, turn and accelerate your shoulders to the mini tramp and release the medicine ball. This exercise can serve as a plyometric drill if you also try and catch the ball. As you get stronger, do not increase the weight of the medicine ball. Instead, increase the distance you need to throw the ball. Look to improve your strength through speed, not by moving a heavier object. Keep in mind that the medicine ball that you are using in the exercise is heavier than a baseball.

Figure 9-24

A Recipe for Success

The normal training principles apply to all of the aforementioned exercises. You still need to incorporate frequency, intensity, and overload into your periodized plan. Keep in mind that for all these exercises, it is not the load that should be your primary focus, but the ability to perform the exercise, using good technique and control on both sides of the body. Because developing rotational strength and endurance through repetition is the desired objective of your training regimen, you should perform three sets of 10-15 repetitions of each exercise.

In your training, you may still do some strength exercises, but only in moderation and as a way of creating a strength base. As you build up your strength in rotation, you need to make sure that whatever gains you achieve are being transferred onto the mound. As a result, you should always ensure you are pitching the right volume of baseballs in practice. Furthermore, whatever pitching you do should be supplemented with the appropriate technical advice from your coach. It is important that any changes that you experience in your ability to exert maximal force through your kinetic chain will become permanent by training the appropriate motor pattern.

While this section has examined prehabilitation training regimens and protocols for increasing the velocity of a pitcher's fastball, another issue that needs to be addressed is what can be done to reestablish a pitcher's ability to throw hard after he has been injured or undergone arm surgery. Section III details the implications of rehabilitating a pitcher's fastball after he has been hurt.

REHABILITATION TRAINING REGIMENS FOR ROTATIONAL MOMENTUM, DIRECTIONAL MOMENTUM, AND RETURN TO HEALTH

Section III

The NPA and many other baseball researchers have known for years that lack of performance with location, movement, velocity, and/or pain/injury are a function of inappropriate mechanical efficiency, functional strength, endurance, flexibility, stamina, and/or pitching workloads (i.e., number of pitches per inning, game, week, month, year). Obviously, it's best when pitchers are prehabilitated or fixed *before* they perform poorly or break down physically. That's what Sections I and II addressed. The fact is, however, pitchers do perform poorly and do get hurt. In that regard, the issue is what can coaches, trainers, conditioning coaches, pitching coaches, and pitchers do to facilitate rehabilitation from pain, injury, and/or a resulting surgery.

For the most part, once a pitcher is out of pain and/or has healed from an injury or surgery, the only difference between prehab and rehab is the level of intensity with his training protocols. Over the years, most baseball medical professionals (physicians, physical therapists, and trainers) have gotten both smarter and better skilled at returning pitchers to form and the field. At the NPA, we wondered what impact our recent research on the biomechanical and physical derivation of real velocity would have on rehab protocols. To find out, the results of our velocity study were forwarded to Alan Tyson, a physical therapist/athletic trainer and vice president of Ortho Carolina Epicenter Sports Performance Center in Charlotte, North Carolina. His thoughts and response to our inquiry are provided in Chapter 10.

10

Velocity Development— Implications for the Rehabilitation of Baseball Pitchers

(Alan Tyson)

The medical community's fascination with the disabled thrower stems from the public admiration of a healthy shoulder and elbow in which velocities upwards of 100 mph can be achieved. Whether the throwing athlete is said to have internal impingement, a SLAP lesion, or anterior instability, the rehabilitation can often be difficult. Returning pre-injury throwing velocity after an injury or surgery is one of the main goals for successful rehabilitation of the shoulder or elbow in a pitcher. Unfortunately, this stage is often the most difficult phase of rehabilitation. In fact, if a pitcher loses as much (or as little) as three-to-four percent of his velocity, he often does not return to his pre-injury level.

At the present time in baseball, a number of pitchers are searching for additional ways to increase velocity by using such means as weighted balls, Jobe rotator-cuff exercises, additional upper-body weight training, etc. Furthermore, leg training has also increased in popularity, since many coaches teach that power in throwing originates from the legs.

Alexander (1998) and Young (1999) have stated that segmental timing of the pelvis, hips, spine, and upper extremity was the most important factor in generating velocity, rather than strength in one individual body part. Mileski (1998) believed that the transfer of energy from the lower extremity to the rotation of the core musculature, combined with the upper-extremity movement, results in maximal velocity. Other studies have looked at upper-extremity mechanics in the throwing motion to determine their effect on velocity (Matsuo 2004, Stodden, 2005). Stodden (2001) was the first to assert that pitchers with higher velocity had increased pelvis and upper-torso orientation angles. This factor is identified as "hip and shoulder separation" by the National Pitching Association.

Rehabilitation Implications

Many pitching coaches have opinions about how velocity is created. The most common philosophy expressed by pitching coaches is that velocity is generated by using the legs, having a very high leg lift, or from pushing off the rubber. The results from a recent study by the National Pitching Association revealed that approximately 79% of the throwing velocity is created by the torque (hip-and-shoulder separation) created in the upper body (hips-to-upper extremity). When the pitchers in the NPA study threw from a kneeling position, no legs were involved in the throwing motion, no slope from the mound to gain momentum, and no leg lift to generate power and/or increase potential energy. Therefore, it can be logically extrapolated that the energy derived from using the legs, throwing off a mound on a downhill slope, and having a leg lift to initiate the throwing motion only contributes 21% to a pitcher's overall velocity.

After a shoulder or elbow injury or following a surgical intervention, it is important to make sure that the pitcher strengthens his lower body. However, the key contributor to velocity development is the torque or hip/shoulder separation. Many studies have focused on upper-extremity mechanics, which has led a number of rehabilitative professionals to conclude that attention to the upper extremity alone would restore velocity. The other assumption that is made is that the more strength in the upper extremity, the more the arm can withstand the stresses of the throwing motion.

On the other hand, given the fact that the results of NPA's investigative efforts have shown that torque development (hip-and-shoulder separation) is the key to developing velocity, it could reasonably be concluded that the emphasis of a pitcher's training should focus on flexibility and core training. As a result, the body would generate more power, and the pitcher would need to use the arm less during the acceleration phase of throwing.

In order to effectively rehabilitate a pitcher, both hip strength and flexibility, along with core or abdominal training, must also be considered. Along with proper mechanical assessment, this step will help ensure that the pitcher can maintain his balance and posture during his delivery, thus maximizing his velocity development. Combining effective rotator cuff and scapulothoracic rehabilitation, with more total-body training, is the recommended approach of the pitcher for returning to his pre-injury status.

Several keys exist for rehabilitating pitchers. In this regard, in addition to his throwing mechanics, the three primary focal areas are: strength in the rotational hip and core muscles, strength and endurance in the posterior scapular muscles, and flexibility about the upper extremity to allow the scapula to move correctly. As such, the following exercises should be considered for inclusion in any pitcher's training regimen.

Rotational Hip and Core Muscle Exercises

While most hip and core exercises that pitchers perform are adequate, most pitchers could improve on the quality and quantity of rotation in their workouts. Remember that it is the torque created by the hip-and-shoulder separation that results in velocity development. The stronger the hip and core muscles are "rotationally," the more power can be developed.

❏ Double-knee balance on the ball with rotation (Figures 10-1 and 10-2): To perform the exercise, start by kneeling on the ball with both knees and placing your hands on the floor. Slowly work your hands from the floor to the ball. Once you achieve a balanced position, sit up in a tall kneeling position. Once you're in a tall-kneeling position, fold your arms across your chest and rotate your upper torso as if to turn into your throwing position. Hold for two-to-three seconds and recover to the start position. Your goal should be able to rotate back and forth for a total of three minutes.

Figure 10-1

Figure 10-2

❏ Trunk rotation (Figures 10-3 and 10-4): Once you have mastered the aforementioned exercise, then attach some Theraband or tubing to a structure and repeat the exercise while having the shoulder in a 90/90 position. As in the previous exercise, your goal should be able to maintain your balance and rotate for three minutes.

Figure 10-3

Figure 10-4

❑ Kick backs (Figures 10-5 to 10-7):
This modified exercise should look familiar to anyone who has seen or taken any type of martial arts. It is applicable to pitchers because it involves balance and hip-rotational strength. Another benefit of this exercise is that it stretches the hamstring on the down leg, which is helpful for a pitcher because it enables him to achieve an easier follow-through on his delivery.

To perform the exercise, start by raising one leg so that your thigh becomes parallel to the floor. With your thigh that is parallel to the floor, rotate it out to the side, while keeping it parallel. From this position, extend your leg behind you, while you lean forward with your upper body. Recover to the start position without putting your foot down. The keys to performing the exercise properly are: keep your thigh level; lean forward as you extend your leg behind you; and finish in a "T" position. Perform two-to-three sets of 10 reps of the exercise.

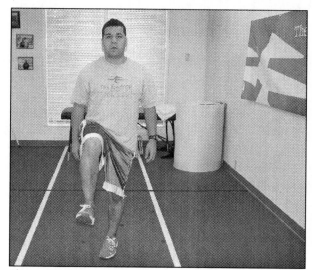

Figure 10-5

Figure 10-6

Figure 10-7

❏ Core—alternating leg lifts on the ball:
Core strength, endurance, and stability are primary factors in velocity development. The ability of the core to control rotation is often overlooked. It is important to note that if the core cannot effectively control rotational forces, then power is lost. Anytime power is diminished about the body, the pitcher either loses velocity or his arm has to work harder to assist in power development.

To perform the exercise, start in a push-up position on the ball. Then, brace your abdominal muscles and slowly lift one leg approximately six inches off the floor. Try not to let your trunk rotate while you alternate lifting each leg from the floor. Repeat for one minute. As this exercise becomes easier, position your hands so that the ball is rolled further out. Then, alternate leg lifts again, holding slightly at the top of each lift. Try to repeat back and forth for one minute.

Upper Back/Scapular Strengthening

A second area of emphasis for the pitcher should be his upper back or scapula muscles. Because of postures that they assume during the day, many individuals have upper back muscles that are not as strong as they should be. Typically, athletes sit to eat, sit to learn, sit to be entertained, etc. Subsequently, when a pitcher throws, he has to get his arm in extremes of motion. If his scapula cannot retract, then his labrum may tear. Eventually, his rotator cuff could tear over time. As a result, the following exercises should be incorporated into a pitcher's upper-body routine at least two-to-three times a week.

❏ "Y" on the ball:

To perform the exercise, assume a position with your chest on the ball and lift your arms up to make the letter "Y." This exercise strengthens the lower trapezius muscle, which helps the shoulder blade move correctly. The keys to doing the exercise properly are to keep the thumbs up and the elbows straight. The exercise should be felt in your upper back, not in front of your shoulders. The exercise should be held for a five-count at the top of the movement. Initially, your goal should be to perform three sets of 10 reps. Eventually, you should work up to being able to do three sets of 20 reps, with a five-lb. dumbbell in each hand (three lbs for pitchers junior high age or younger).

❏ "T" on the ball:

To perform the exercise, assume a position with your chest on the ball and lift your arms up to make the letter "T." This exercise strengthens the middle trapezius, rhomboid, and rotator cuff muscles, which help the shoulder blade move correctly. The keys to doing the exercise properly are to keep the thumbs up and the elbows straight. The exercise should be felt in your upper back, not in front of your shoulders. The exercise should be held for a five-count at the top of the movement. Initially, your goal should be to perform three sets of 10 reps. Eventually, you should work up to being able to do three sets of 20 reps, while holding a five-lb dumbbell in each hand (three lbs for pitchers junior high age or younger).

❏ "Bent T" on the ball:

To perform the exercise, assume a position with your chest on the ball and lift your arms up to make a "bent T." This exercise strengthens the middle trapezius, rhomboids, and rotator cuff muscles, which help the shoulder blade move correctly. The keys to doing the exercise properly are to keep your palms down and your elbows bent. The exercise should be felt in your upper back, not in front of your shoulders. The exercise should be held for a five-count at the to of the movement. Your goal should be to perform three sets of 10 reps. Eventually, you should work up to being able to do three sets of 20 reps, while holding a five-lb dumbbell in each hand (three lbs for pitchers junior high age or younger).

❏ Hummingbird:

This exercise challenges the strength and endurance of the posterior shoulder-blade muscles. The exercise involves positioning the arm to simulate the later cocking phase of throwing. Positioning the arm in the extreme of external rotation, the athlete is asked to oscillate in a small but quick arc, much like the quickness of a hummingbird's wings.

In order to perform the exercise, tie a knot in one end of a Theraband, place it over the top of the door, and close the door. Grab the Theraband and position your shoulder to achieve a 90-degree angle. Your elbow should also be bent at a 90-degree angle. While maintaining your shoulder and elbow at 90 degrees, rotate your arm backward and perform a small, quick oscillating movement. The player should try to perform this small oscillatory movement as fast as possible, somewhat like a hummingbird flapping his small wings.

Flexibility

Three key areas that are often restricted in pitchers are the forearms, posterior capsule, and latissimus dorsi. Tightness in either of these areas can cause extra stress on your elbow and shoulder during the throwing motion. As such, the following stretches should be incorporated into a pitcher's daily conditioning/training routine.

❏ Latissimus and upper-back stretch:
To perform the exercise, lean against a table or edge of a bed with your elbows together. Then, lean back with your hips going towards your heels. Let your upper back relax and "sag." The key to doing the exercise properly is to keep your elbows together. You should feel the stretch in your upper back or lat area. You should not feel any discomfort in your shoulders. Your goal should be to perform three sets of the exercise for 30 seconds.

❏ Latissimus stretch:
This stretch is a variation of the previous exercise. After assuming the "sag" position noted in the previous stretch, keep your elbows together and "round" your back. You know you are performing the stretch correctly when the tension increases in the latissimus region. Your goal should be to perform three sets of the exercise for 30 seconds.

❏ Posterior capsule stretch:
To perform the exercise, lie on your side, with your shoulder and elbow positioned at a 90-degree angle. Turn slightly off your side so that you are not lying directly on your shoulder. Maintaining your shoulder and elbow at 90 degrees, position your opposite hand around your wrist and gently push your wrist and forearm down towards the table. You should feel the stretch in the back of your shoulder. Make sure that you do not lie directly on your side. You should feel the stretch in the back of your shoulder. You should not allow your shoulder to rise off the table. Your goal should be to perform three sets of the exercise for 30 seconds.

❏ Forearm stretch:
To perform the exercise, position your hand on a table so that your forearm is facing in a forward direction and your fingers are pointing directing behind. If you have trouble with your wrist reaching the table or if the stretch is uncomfortable, then place a small folded towel under the edge of the heel of your hand. Make sure your fingers are completely on the table and are as straight as possible. To increase the stretch, rotate your body away from the forearm being stretched. Make sure that your elbow is as straight as possible

and that your fingers are straight behind your forearm. Rotate your body to increase the stretch. Your goal should be to perform three sets of the exercise for one minute each.

Postscript

Obviously, a lot of similarities exist in the prehab exercises detailed in Section II and the rehab exercises described in Section III. In fact, the protocols could be interchangeable *if* volume, load, frequency, intensity, and duration of work (especially intensity) are performed to tolerance as the athlete recovers and repairs from his injury or surgery. The next section, Section IV, provides an overview of the final piece of the NPA's recommended training to develop real velocity.

VELOCITY ENHANCEMENT PROTOCOLS: IMPROVING PHYSICAL/BIOMECHANICAL ENERGY SEQUENCING AND ARM SPEED

Section IV

The first three sections of this book were written to explain and detail new protocols for training rotational strength, endurance, stability, mobility, and flexibility in the legs/core/upper body, which we believe are the foundation of real velocity. This section focuses on "cracking the whip," literally, with information and instruction on how maximize "pure" arm speed.

The sequencing of kinetic links and arm speed occurs when the forearm moves from external into internal rotation, snapping straight into the release point, timing, and imparting optimal energy and maximum velocity onto a baseball. Our discussions with Greg Rose at TPI have enabled us to achieve a better understanding of why kinematic sequencing and kinetic energy translation in the throwing arm are improved by performing skill movements with baseballs/bats/clubs that are 20% heavier/lighter than competitively weighted baseballs/bats/clubs. This objective is achieved by maximizing the neuromuscular interaction of a throw/swing around four basic factors: the structural stability of the joint/bone; the mobility of the plastic stabilizers (rotator cuff/labrum/cartilage); flexibility of the elastic conduits (fascia, tendons, ligaments); and the efficiency of energy recruitment and availability (nerve synapse/fast-twitch muscle fiber).

Consistent results were found between the original overload/underload implement weight-training study for pitchers/hitters conducted in 1987-1988 by Coop DeRenne (University of Hawaii) and Tom House (Texas Rangers

Baseball Club) and the velocity study recently undertaken by the NPA concerning the following:

- Throwing an overloaded, six-ounce (heavier by one ounce) baseball helped increase strength/endurance/flexibility in structure, plastic stabilizers, and elastic conduits without adversely affecting the pitcher's mechanics or joint health.

- Throwing an underloaded, four-ounce baseball increased both arm speed and five-ounce ball velocity by having a positive impact on the elastic conduits and energy availability/recruitment with the nerves and fast-twitch muscle fibers, again without adversely affecting the pitcher's mechanics or joint health.

During the studies, several other interesting phenomena were also observed concerning how the body subconsciously accommodates even small (one ounce) weight differences, when pitching with four-, five-, and six-ounce baseballs, for example:

- Arm path and stride had the same "signature" route (refer to Chapter 1) with all three different weights. On the other hand, the throwing arm and stride foot traveled further with the four-ounce ball and shorter with the six-ounce ball, when measured and compared with the arm path/stride length when throwing a five-ounce ball.

- Likewise, when compared to throwing a five-ounce baseball, less north/south, east/west posture changes occurred when throwing a four-ounce ball than when using a six-ounce ball.

- Finally, comparing torque when throwing a five-ounce ball showed that more hip-and-shoulder separation occurred with the six-ounce ball, and less hip-and-shoulder separation occurred with the four-ounce ball.

Obviously, the body is incredibly fine-tuned to handle the violent movements involved in a pitcher's delivery. In reality, the body will find a posture and torque in which it can stabilize while throwing. It's a "posture paradox," because no matter in what posture a pitcher starts, his body will ultimately find a posture that it's strong enough to provide him with the necessary support. Also, the pitcher's arm path will shorten/lengthen, depending on the weight of the implement relative to his strength, stability, mobility, and flexibility.

The following brief, but important, digression provides some further insight concerning how a thrower's body will match his strength to accommodate the weight of any implement. Initially, pitchers doing the towel drill (two-to-three ounces) had the same biomechanical signature as they did with a baseball (five ounces), but a slightly longer arm path and stride. The same observation held true with stride length and arm path length and a four-ounce ball—longer than a five-ounce ball, but shorter than a two- to- three-ounce towel. Conversely, pitchers throwing a six-ounce ball had less stride and arm path than they did with a standard five-ounce ball.

In reality, a quarterback throwing a deep pattern pass with a football (15 ounces) has the same biomechanical signature as a pitcher, but with a shorter arm path and less stride. It should be noted that the longest stride we could observe with a quarterback was 24 inches (± two inches or ~ 1/3 of the normal 72 inches ± two-inch stride pitchers take). In other words, a six-foot quarterback throwing a 15-ounce implement at maximum effort had a two-foot stride. On the other hand, a six-foot pitcher throwing a five-ounce implement at maximum effort had a six-foot stride.

The aforementioned statistic would seem to indicate that within its biomechanical structure and strength capabilities, the body's arm path and stride length react inversely proportional to the weight of the implement. However, we were pleasantly surprised to discover that when our pitchers successfully completed their SUV programs, stride length and arm path length were virtually the same with a six-ounce, four-ounce, and four-ounce ball, as well as with a two-to-three ounce towel. In other words, ± 20% of competitive implement, every link in the body of the study's subjects had been functionally trained with enough useable strength, stability, mobility, and flexibility to support the total-body stress of each pitch/delivery.

Finally, the only true "power" movement in the kinetic chain of a pitcher's delivery (by definition, $1/2 \ m \ x \ v^2$) is his throwing forearm, wrist, and hand, which accelerate the baseball into its release point. After foot strike, it's the only energy link in the chain where it's more about weight, distance, and *time* than *timing*. Rather, the key factor is the availability of efficient/effective energy and the recruitment of energy to the throwing forearm than total-body rotational, directional momentum. It's also the one segment of the body in which muscle fiber can be influenced and/or enhanced.

The aforementioned leads into a discussion on implement weight training and what the research has revealed about velocity enhancement. In this regard, Chapters 11-13 summarize the testing methodology, implementation, and quantification from a representative sample of past/present cross-specific velocity studies. Collectively, these studies help explain the evolution of implement training.

In the interest of full disclosure, it should be noted that these studies were conducted using weighted baseballs from Diamond Baseball and Decker Sports. Subsequently, the velocity improvement program (Diamond Baseball) and the Velocity Development Protocol (Decker Sports) became products that both of these companies marketed to pitchers and coaches. Chapters 11-13 also include some written material provided by each company.

11

Throwing Velocity Study: Comparing Two Integral Weighted-Implement Training Programs

(Coop DeRenne and Tom House)

1985 – 1986

In 1985, Tom House and Coop DeRenne began combining forces. With our baseball influence and our positive research results, we were able to convince Diamond Sports Company to manufacture the four ounce underloaded baseball for the 1986 project. Identical to the high quality, bests-selling, five-ounce D-1 Diamond baseball, the four-ounce underloaded baseballs were experimental, uniformly balanced, and weighed.

Thirty-four high school pitchers participated in this 1986 fall seasonal study that involved an underloaded throwing project. The volunteered pitchers were randomly divided into two research groups. The results of this study supported the positive findings of the previous 1982 and 1984 projects. Significant differences (P≤.05) were found between the pre- and-post- test velocity scores. Group # 1, training with the underloaded four-ounce, and the standard five-ounce baseballs, gained on average 2.6 mph in velocity. The velocity of the subjects in group #2, the controlled group that didn't train with the underloaded baseballs (they only threw the five-ounce standard baseballs) decreased 1/2 mph over the course of the 10-week study.

The study showed that training with underloaded baseballs significantly increased arm velocities. Again, for the third consecutive project, the experimental training produced no arm injuries.

The results of the 1986 study, along with the investigative efforts conducted over the previous six years that involved weighted-implement training projects with bats and baseballs validated the specificity of training principle. Given the results of these projects and the findings of several studies that were conducted in the Soviet Union during this period, a decision was made to conduct two additional throwing projects. In turn, the Diamond Sports Company agreed to manufacture and package the overloaded six-ounce baseball with the underloaded four-ounce baseball.

The next two studies (conducted in 1987 and 1988) would prove to be the final phase in the evolutionary process involving our envestigative efforts on throwing. This final phase consisted of subjects exercising with the combination (integral training) of the underloaded and overloaded four- and six-ounce baseballs. In our opinion, exercising with the weighted baseballs in a precise integral weight-training program would produce the following:

• Neurological changes that may increase the number of muscle fibers recruited (thereby increasing arm speed). The weights of the baseballs used in tandem would allow the thrower to exert maximum force through the whole range of motion at high velocities, thereby resulting in more fast-twitch fibers (Type IIB) being recruited. As a result of that recruitment, some combination of force and velocity would be produced.

• Neurological changes that may improve the synchronization of muscle contractions (neuromuscular memory). During the integral-training process, each subject duplicates his throwing arm's range of motion movements with greater speeds than his competitive speed. Therefore, the timing of the muscle fibers' activation (firing) would be maintained, with no loss of coordination. On the other hand, the rate of firing would be increased.

As a consequence of the aforementioned two neurologic changes—the enhancement of muscle fiber activation and recruitment, we felt that increases in the speed-strength capabilities of the throwing arm would occur during the integral weighted-implement program.

Based on his own research findings, L.A. Vasiliev (1983), when discussing the production of speed-strength capabilities, concluded, "the most effective force was found in those combinations in which the light and heavier weights differed the least from the standard weight." The key word in Vasiliev's conclusion is *combination*.

The primary objectives of the next two integral, combination, or mixed weighted-baseball throwing projects (conducted initially in 1987 and then repeated in 1988) were to determine the proper training sequences when employing weighted baseballs and the appropriate pitch ratios of the weighted baseballs. A decision was made to increase the sample sizes in our study to include high school, junior college, and university-level competitive pitchers.

1987

The 1987 underloaded and overloaded throwing project incorporated the integration of both the light- and heavy-weighted baseballs into an integral throwing program. Forty-one high school pitchers and 70 university-level pitchers participated in the study, which was conducted over a 10-week period in the fall. A university-level test group was included in the throwing project in order to determine if positive results could be obtained with a different age group. Each age-group division involved three research groups. Statistically, significant differences were found between the three groups (P≤.05).

Group #1 threw the weighted baseballs in the standard-heavy-light-standard sequence for the entire 10 weeks. In the high school division, group #1 averaged velocity gains of 4.4 mph. Group #1 in the university-level division achieved average velocity gains of 3.8 mph.

Group #2 threw the weighted baseballs in the standard-heavy-standard sequence for five weeks and in the standard-light-standard sequence for the remaining five weeks. In the high school division, group #2 averaged velocity gains of 4.4 mph. In the university-level division, group #2 achieved average velocity gains of 2.9 mph. Statistically (P≤.05), groups #1 and #2 increased their velocities significantly.

The controlled group in both the high school and university-level divisions did not throw with the weighted baseballs. The average gains of the high school and university-level pitchers in group #3 were .9 mph and -2.8 mph, respectively.

Similar to previous studies, no arm injuries occurred during this project, which is the most important constant result that we have found throughout the entire evolution of weighted-implement training.

The importance of the finds of the 1987 study lies in two significant areas:
- Establishing the training sequences for weighted baseballs
- Establishing pitch ratios for the weighted baseballs

Given that members of both groups #1 and #2 experienced significant velocity increases, it was found that both weighted-baseball training sequences produced meaningful improvement in throwing velocity. Accordingly, a pitcher has a choice of selecting which weighted-baseball sequence to use in his training: the six-, four-, five-ounce (heavy-light-standard); or six-, five-ounce for the first half of the training period (heavy-standard) and then the four-, five-ounce (light-standard) sequence for the last half of the training period.

The Soviets obtained positive training results, using different weight sequences with the light-heavy-standard shot puts. Their research supports the findings of our throwing projects that involved employing two different weight sequences.

The 1987 study also showed that the pitch ratios of the weighted baseballs (i.e., the ratio of the number of pitches thrown with each weighted baseball) contributed to the significant velocity gains that were achieved by groups #1 and #2. As supported by the findings of the Soviet studies, our study involved throwing the light and heavy baseballs twice as many times as the standard five-ounce baseball. The ratio of pitches increased throughout the entire training period, as follows:

- 1:2:2:1 for standard-heavy-light-standard sequence (5 oz.-6 oz.-4 oz.-5 oz.)
- 1:2:1: for standard-heavy-standard, standard-light-standard sequence (5 oz.-6 oz.-5 oz. for the first half of the training period; and 5 oz.-4 oz.-5 oz. for last half of the training period)

Our research results support the conclusion that particular weighted-baseballs training sequences, used in tandem with the proper weighted-baseball pitch ratios, will increase pitching velocity. Analyses of these findings indicate that such significant velocity gains are a function of physiological and neurological (neuromuscular memory) conditioning.

Based on the 1982, 1984, 1986, and 1987 research study findings that showed that velocity increases resulted from the use of weighted baseballs, Diamond Sports Company manufactured the first of four- and six-ounce weighted baseballs that were available to the public to purchase commercially. The baseballs were sold under the trade name, The Tom House V.I.P. (Velocity Improvement Plan). The precise guideline-training program used in the NPA's research projects was included in the packaging for each weighted baseball.

1988

In 1988, we duplicated the 1987 integral V.I.P. throwing study in order to confirm the velocity gains of the 1987 project and prove beyond a shadow of a doubt that the weight-load sequence and pitch ratios of the four-, five, and six-ounce weighted baseballs were correct. In other words, our goal was to verify the efficiency of the V.I.P. velocity program and to reconfirm the fact that engaging in the V.I.P. program would not lead to arm injuries.

Conducted in the fall of 1988, the new study involved 110 university-level pitchers who participated in the underload/overload weighted-implement throwing project. Similar to the results of the 1987 project, statistically ($P \leq .05$) significant differences were found between the research groups. The experimental groups #1 and #2 that trained with the weighted baseballs and followed the weighted-implement training program (V.I.P.) increased their velocities significantly.

Group #1 threw the weighted baseballs in the standard-heavy-light-standard sequence for the entire 10 weeks. The program for group #1 proved to be as effective as in the 1987 project. Group #1's average velocity gains were 3 mph.

Group #2 threw the weighted baseballs initially in the standard-heavy-standard sequence for five weeks and then in the standard-light-standard sequence for the remaining five weeks. As in the 1987 project, this program proved to be highly effective. Group #2's average velocity gains were 2.6 mph.

The controlled group #3 did not throw weighted baseballs. They threw only the standard five-ounce baseball during their bullpen experiences. Group #3 had average velocity loss of .3 mph.

Summary

The results of the 1988 project support and confirm the findings of the 1987 study. A total of 221 pitchers participated in the two integral weighted-implements training throwing (V.I.P.) projects. The two experimental groups that threw the weighted baseballs significantly increased their throwing velocities. The controlled group pitchers did not show any velocity gains during the experimental period. Not a single experimental pitcher suffered an arm injury while participating in these projects. Accordingly, it can reasonably be concluded that during the fall off-season, pitchers can increase their velocities, while training precisely with the V.I.P. program under the careful "eye" of a monitoring pitching coach. Equally as important, the possibility of sustaining an arm injury while V.I.P. training is very remote or practically negligible.

Research Protocol for the 1987 Integral Project

❑ Purpose: To compare the impact of two integral weighted-implement training programs on throwing velocity

❑ Subjects:
   <u>41 high school pitchers</u>
   • Group #1: Heavy-light-standard sequence
   • Group #2: Heavy-standard; light-standard
   • Group #3: Control

   <u>70 university-level pitchers</u>
   • Group #1: Heavy-light-standard sequence
   • Group #2: Heavy-standard; light-standard
   • Group #3: Control

❑ Implements: Underloaded four-ounce baseball; overloaded six-ounce baseball; standard five-ounce baseball

- ❏ Measuring device: RAGUN electromagnetic radar

- ❏ Results: Significant increases (P≤.05). Group #1—4.4 mph and 3.8 mph gains, respectively; group #2—4.4 mph and 2.9 mph gains, respectively; group #3—.9 mph gain and -2.8 mph loss, respectively.

Research Protocol for the 1988 Replication Study of the 1987 Project

- ❏ Purpose: To determine the effects of two integral weighted-implement training programs on throwing velocity

- ❏ Subjects:
  110 university-level pitchers
  - Group #1: Heavy-light-standard sequence
  - Group #2: Heavy-standard; light-standard
  - Group #3: Control group

- ❏ Implements: Underloaded four-ounce baseball; overloaded six-ounce baseball; standard five-ounce baseball

- ❏ Measuring device: RAGUN electromagnetic radar

- ❏ Results: significant increases (P≤.05); group #1, 3 mph gains; group #2, 2.6 mph gains; 4) Group 3, 3 mph loss

Training Schedule and the Weights of the Ball Used in the 1987 and 1988 Training Projects

Treatment Group (University Subject)	1 to 5 Week	6 to 10 Week
I (n = 60)	5 oz-6 oz 4 oz-5 oz	5 oz-6 oz 4 oz-5 oz
II (n = 60)	5 oz-6 oz-5 oz	5 oz-4 oz-5 oz
III (n = 60)	5 oz	5 oz

I: Integral program I

II: Integral program II

III: Control group

Lesson-Plan Structure for the 1987 and 1988 Projects

Treatment Group (University Study)	No. of Sessions Per Week	Week	No. of Ptiches Per Session	No. and Sequence of Pitching with Different Weighted Ball in Season
I (n = 60)	3	1-3	54	Stan.-Overwt.-Underwt.-Stan. (9) (18) (18) (9)
	3	4-6	60	Stan.-Overwt.-Underwt.-Stan. (10) (20) (20) (10)
	3	7-8	66	Stan.-Overwt.-Underwt.-Stan. (11) (22) (22) (11)
	3	9-10	75	Stan.-Overwt.-Underwt.-Stan. (12) (25) (25) (13)
II (n = 60)	3	1-3	54	Standard-Overweight-Standard (9) (36) (9)
	3	4-5	60	Standard-Overweight-Standard (10) (40) (10)
	3	6	60	Standard-Underweight-Standard (10) (40) (10)
	3	7-8	66	Standard-Underweight-Standard (11) (44) (11)
	3	9-10	75	Standard-Underweight-Standard (12) (50) (13)
III (n = 60)	3	1-3	54	Standard – (54)
	3	4-6	60	Standard – (60)
	3	7-8	66	Standard – (66)
	3	9-10	75	Standard – (75)

I: Integral program I

II: Integral program II

III: Control group

Throwing Velocity Prior to and Post the 10 Weeks of Training with Overweighted, Underweighted, and Standard Balls (1987 and 1988)

Treatment Group University Subject	Prior to Training (mph)	Post Training (mph)	Gain Score (mph)
I (n = 60)	77.02 ± 3.72	80.24 ± 3.59	3.22 ± 1.57 **
II (n = 60)	76.50 ± 4.07	79.23 ± 4.14	2.72 ± 1.70 **
III (n = 60)	76.39 ± 4.11	76.29 ± 4.03	-0.16 ± 1.13

I: Integral program I

II: Integral program II

III: Control group

Gain score: difference between prior to and post training

All values are means, with ± standard deviations noted.

** Significant Newman-Keuls contrasts (P≤.05)

The Original Tom House VIP Diamond Velocity Improvement Plan

❑ *Implement weight training* (the ball is the implement)

❑ *Improve arm speed* (by improving neuromuscular interaction)

❑ *Throw harder* (through improved neuromuscular memory)

❑ *Throw farther* (through improved neuromuscular memory)

❑ *For use by pitchers and all other players*

> Before beginning this program, read this entire
> instructional guide with your coach and/or parents.
> Recommended for ages 15 years and up.

Other strength programs employ barbells, dumbbells, and/or a variety of machines and utilize a variety of biomechanical actions and angles. Only the V.I.P. program uses an actual baseball as the training implement. The green (four-ounce) baseball allows you to increase your arm speed, while the black (six-ounce) baseball can help you develop neuromuscular strength.

The use of these two balls, in combination with a regular five-ounce baseball, will enable you to train, while employing the same body action, arm route, velocity, and competitive energy as would normally be employed during a game. Thus, the transfer of your training effect to game situations will be at the highest level of efficiency.

How to Use the V.I.P.

V.I.P. TERMINOLOGY:

❑ V.I.P. stands for velocity improvement plan.

❑ *Bullpen workout, skill workout, and side-work* all have the same meaning.

❑ *V.I.P. baseballs*:
  • Black six-ounce V.I.P. baseball
  • Green four-ounce V.I.P. baseball
  • A regular five-ounce Diamond baseball

❑ *Mechanical efficiency* occurs when your arm and body allow you to use your normal stride, arm arc, arm angle, release point, and follow-through.

❑ *To tolerance* is that point where you can maintain pain-free mechanical efficiency.

❑ *Aerobic work* refers to engaging in activities such as running, jogging, sprints, jump rope activities, stationary bicycle, etc.

❑ *Ratio* indicates the comparative number of times an individual actually throws each of the V.I.P balls during any one V.I.P. workout.

❑ *Sequence* refers to the order in which the four-, five-, and six-ounce balls are thrown. The regular five-ounce ball should always be thrown both first and last in every V.I.P. bullpen/skill workout. The sequence should always be: five-ounce ball first, six-ounce ball next, then the four-ounce ball, and the five-ounce ball last.

THE V.I.P. WORKOUT:
The V.I.P workout consists of three parts. You should "loosen up" to "warm up" to do the "V.I.P. bullpen/skill workout."

❑ Loosen up (period of 8-to-10 minutes):
Start with three-to-five minutes of aerobic activity. Do appropriate calisthenics and stretching exercises for the remainder of the loosening-up period. If possible, wear flat-soled exercise shoes.

❑ Warm up (period of 8-to-10 minutes):
Do another three-to-five minutes of aerobic activity. Then, do short toss/long toss for the remainder of the warm-up period. Use only the regular five-ounce baseball for throwing. Perform this stage on a flat surface, not on the mound. If possible, wear flat-soled exercise shoes.

❑ V.I.P. bullpen/skill workout (period of 8-to-10 minutes for first three weeks):
After three weeks of consistent workouts, you may need to increase this stage to 10-to-12 minutes.

Before each V.I.P. workout, the coach and player should collectively determine the total number of pitches to be made during that particular workout. Stay with that number for that workout unless a factor such as darkness, rain, or fatigue, etc. prohibits completing the predetermined number of pitches. The number of predetermined pitches can vary from workout to workout.

Select a ratio from any of the enclosed ratio charts (A to F), based upon your predetermined total number of pitches for that day. Proceed moderately. Do not advance more than one line per workout. During the first three weeks of your training, stay under 50 total pitches per day. All ratios are designed to provide the same optimal neuromuscular training.

Proceed with your throws or pitches from the ratio you have selected by reading across the ratio line. Always follow the proper sequence.

Expect a certain lack of control with the six-ounce and four-ounce balls during your first three weeks of training. Focus on maximizing arm speed with good mechanics, not on your control. Your control will improve as you continue your workouts.

When switching from the five-ounce ball to the six-ounce ball, take five medium-speed throws to allow your fingers to adjust to the new ball weight. Do not count any medium-speed throws towards your ratio. When going from the six-ounce ball to the four-ounce ball, and from the four-ounce to the last round of the five-ounce ball, again take five medium-speed throws before you start to count your ratio throws.

SPECIAL V.I.P. INSTRUCTIONS FOR PITCHERS:
A pitcher should use only the regular five-ounce Diamond baseballs on game day or the day before a game. For example, if you are scheduled to pitch on a Friday, your V.I.P. skills workout should occur on a Tuesday or Wednesday, not on a Thursday or Friday.

The actual V.I.P. pitching workout should be done on a mound away from the regular game mound, if possible. This workout should be done at the regulation pitching distance, using the same timing, rhythm, body action, and arm speed as during actual competition. Keep this side work clean and quick, not over-communicated and drawn out. Wear regular baseball shoes.

Only throw fastballs with the six-ounce and four-ounce balls. Use the regular five-ounce Diamond ball to throw curve balls, breaking balls, change-ups, and other pitches, as well as the fastball.

SPECIAL V.I.P. INSTRUCTIONS FOR POSITION PLAYERS:
Position players should do their V.I.P. work on a flat surface, at a distance of about 10-to-15 feet longer than the distance from home plate to first base. Two players can train with each other at the same time, using proper throwing mechanics from the standing position used by players when they play catch. Wear regular baseball shoes.

If you take fielding practice accompanied by throwing, have the fielding practice come just before the V.I.P. workout, because it will take the place of the loosen-up and warm-up phases.

Do not take outfield and infield practice early. Take an hour off for batting practice and then come back and do the loosen-up and warm-up phases. It would be very hard to prepare the body for a successful V.I.P. workout with this type of workout plan.

IMPORTANT:
Take precautions to prevent the V.I.P. baseballs from getting wet, because water absorption may adversely affect their weight. Immediately replace any V.I.P. ball that has absorbed water. The V.I.P. balls are designed with specific weights, which must be maintained in order to achieve the desired training results and to avoid injury.

The V.I.P. baseballs should be thrown only whenever a player is working on his mechanical skills during a V.I.P. bullpen/skill workout. The V.I.P. baseballs should not be used on game day. Pre-game activities and warm-ups should be done using the regular five-ounce Diamond baseball.

The quantitative makeup of each pitching workout is a decision that should collectively be made by both the coach and the pitcher, with regard to the number of pitches and/or the frequency of pitching workouts per week. However, never use the V.I.P. baseballs for more than 80 pitches/throws per day or for more than 180 pitches/throws per week in any combination of ratios.

The V.I.P. bullpen/skill workout should be the last throwing done by an athlete on a particular day. If further aerobic activity is needed that day, it should be done as soon as possible after the V.I.P. workout.

You do not have to reach the last line of any ratio chart in any specified period of time, if ever! Settle in on the ratio chart and line number that best meets your style of workout. On the other hand, if you occasionally try the same line number on a different ratio chart, it may help prevent "workout staleness." For example, your best workout seems to be ratio chart "A" line number "8." After repeating ratio chart A, line 8 for three or four consecutive workouts, you might try doing ratio chart B or C, line 8 as an alternate workout.

RATIO CHART A

Line	Total Pitches	Pitches With 5 oz.	Pitches With 6 oz.	Pitches With 4 oz.	Pitches With 5 oz.
1	18	3	3	6	6
2	24	4	4	8	8
3	30	5	5	10	10
4	36	6	6	12	12
5	42	7	7	14	14
6	48	8	8	16	16
7	54	9	9	18	18
8	60	10	10	20	20
9	66	11	11	22	22
10	72	12	12	24	24
11	78	13	13	26	26

RATIO CHART B

Line	Total Pitches	Pitches With 5 oz.	Pitches With 6 oz.	Pitches With 4 oz.	Pitches With 5 oz.
1	18	3	6	3	6
2	24	4	8	4	8
3	30	5	10	5	10
4	36	6	12	6	12
5	42	7	14	7	14
6	48	8	16	8	16
7	54	9	18	9	18
8	60	10	20	10	20
9	66	11	22	11	22
10	72	12	24	12	24
11	78	13	26	13	26

RATIO CHART C

Line	Total Pitches	Pitches With 5 oz.	Pitches With 6 oz.	Pitches With 4 oz.	Pitches With 5 oz.
1	18	3	6	6	3
2	24	4	8	8	4
3	30	5	10	10	5
4	36	6	12	12	6
5	42	7	14	14	7
6	48	8	16	16	8
7	54	9	18	18	9
8	60	10	20	20	10
9	66	11	22	22	11
10	72	12	24	24	12
11	78	13	26	26	13

RATIO CHART D

Line	Total Pitches	Pitches With 5 oz.	Pitches With 6 oz.	Pitches With 4 oz.	Pitches With 5 oz.
1	21	6	3	6	6
2	28	8	4	8	8
3	35	10	5	10	10
4	42	12	6	12	12
5	49	14	7	14	14
6	56	16	8	16	16
7	63	18	9	18	18
8	70	20	10	20	20
9	77	22	11	22	22

RATIO CHART E

Line	Total Pitches	Pitches With 5 oz.	Pitches With 6 oz.	Pitches With 4 oz.	Pitches With 5 oz.
1	21	6	6	3	6
2	28	8	8	4	8
3	35	10	10	5	10
4	42	12	12	6	12
5	49	14	14	7	14
6	56	16	16	8	16
7	63	18	18	9	18
8	70	20	20	10	20
9	77	22	22	11	22

RATIO CHART F

Line	Total Pitches	Pitches With 5 oz.	Pitches With 6 oz.	Pitches With 4 oz.	Pitches With 5 oz.
1	21	6	6	6	3
2	28	8	8	8	4
3	35	10	10	10	5
4	42	12	12	12	6
5	49	14	14	14	7
6	56	16	16	16	8
7	63	18	18	18	9
8	70	20	20	20	10
9	77	22	22	22	11

12

Omaha Central High School 2004 Baseball Velocity Study

(Jerry Kreber)

Overview

The study involved a 9-week program that integrated the use of underweight and overweight balls, along with performing dry mechanical drills for pitchers that are designed to improve velocity, endurance, and techniques during the pitching delivery. Table 12-1 presents an overview of the test results for the subjects in the study.

Participants:

Eight individuals participated in the study, from 15-to-18 years old. The age of each participant was as follows:

Player #1: 18 years old   Player #5: 16 years old

Player #2: 17 years old   Player #6: 16 years old

Player #3: 17 years old   Player #7: 15 years old

Player #4: 17 years old   Player #8: 17 years old

Procedures:

Each player was assigned a throwing partner at the beginning of the program and given a set of Decker Sports weighted balls, which consisted of a set of four-ounce, five-ounce, and six-ounce baseballs to be thrown three times per week. An initial training session was held to instruct players on how to perform the drills and throwing progressions involved in the program. Each member of the program was required to attend the orientation meeting. The workouts were unsupervised. The program relied on the honesty of each player to help chart his progress.

Name	Baseline	Test 2	Test 3	Final Test	Diff.	PR
Player 1	82 mph	87 mph	90 mph	90 mph	+8	90
Player 2	85 mph	84 mph	87 mph	87 mph	+2	60
Player 3	76 mph	79 mph	81 mph	82 mph	+6	90
Player 4	79 mph	83 mph	84 mph	84 mph	+5	60
Player 5	76 mph	80 mph	84 mph	84 mph	+8	75
Player 6	84 mph	84 mph	84 mph	84 mph	NC	75
Player 7	76 mph	76 mph	76 mph	77 mph	+1	60
Player 8	76 mph	79 mph	78 mph	76 mph	+3	20
PR = Participation rate with program, measured as a percentage						

Table 12-1. Individual test results

Overall Results:
- Average gain for program: 4.125 mph (includes all participants)
- Average gain for program: 4.29 mph (includes seven participants)
- Average gain for program: 4.86 mph (includes six participants)
- Average participation rate: 63.75% (includes all participants)

Discussion:
In the previous section, the results of the study were grouped into three different levels. The first total includes all eight of the program's participants. The second tabulation includes seven participants, while the third total includes six of the individuals who engaged in the program. The scores were separated because player #7 dropped out of the study after three weeks. Although he did not continue the workouts, he still showed up to be tested. Subsequently, player #8 stopped participating in the program after five weeks. In order to provide accurate results, a sum total for the six participants who competed in the program for the whole 9-week period was calculated.

The results of the six participants showed that a significant increase in their throwing velocity occurred. The average gain for each pitcher was 4.86 mph. Players #1 and #5 had the biggest gain in velocity, with an 8 mph improvement. Player #3 had the second biggest improvement at 6 mph. In addition, players #4 and #2 achieved an increase of 5 and 2 mph, respectively. For whatever reason, player #6 did not improve his velocity over the 9-week program.

Maximum velocity was not the only improvement increased during this program. Players experienced an improvement in their level of velocity endurance as well. For example, player #1, in his final testing period, was able to hit 88 mph on the radar gun seven times during his throwing session. Player #2, who saw only a 2-mph improvement, was able to register 87 mph on the radar gun three times during his last bullpen routine. Moreover, player #4 was able to register 84 mph four times during his final testing session. These scores represented a significant improvement over the initial baseline measurement of the study's participants.

Finally, the average gain for players who had a participation rate (PR) of 75% or more was 5.5 mph. This average includes player #6, who experienced no gain at all during the program. If the results of player #6 were subtracted, the average gain for players who participated in the program 75% of the time would be an astounding 7.7 mph.

Omaha Central Baseball 9-Week Weighted Ball Workout

❑ Monday:
  • 5-minute jog
  • Form running—two sets of each activity:
    ✓ high knees
    ✓ shuffle
    ✓ hip flex
    ✓ carioca
    ✓ stride outs
  • Weighted-ball workout

❑ Tuesday – (NPA drills; no ball required):
  • Cross-arms drill
  • Glove-side drill
  • Equal/opposite-check drill
  • Cross-over drill
  • Total-body towel drill
  • Torque-towel drill
  • Gloved-towel drill
  • Step or bucket drill
  • Flat-back drill

❑ Wednesday:
  • 5-minute jog
  • Form running—two sets of each activity:
    ✓ high knees
    ✓ shuffle
    ✓ hip flex
    ✓ carioca
    ✓ stride outs
  • Weighted-ball workout

- ❏ Thursday – (NPA drills; no ball required):
  - Cross-arms drill
  - Glove-side drill
  - Equal/opposite-check drill
  - Cross-over drill
  - Total-body towel drill
  - Torque-towel drill
  - Gloved-towel drill
  - Step or bucket drill
  - Flat-back drill

- ❏ Friday:
  - 5-minute jog
  - Form running—two sets of each activity:
    - ✓ high knees ✓ carioca
    - ✓ shuffle ✓ stride-outs
    - ✓ hip flex
  - Weighted-ball workout

- ❏ Weighted-ball workout totals:

			Sequence of Throws
• Week 1-2	MWF	Total Throws 54	9-18-18-9 (R-O-U-R)
• Week 3-4	MWF	Total Throws 60	10-20-20-10 (R-O-U-R)
• Week 5-6	MWF	Total Throws 66	11-22-22-11 (R-O-U-R)
• Week 7-8	MWF	Total Throws 72	12-24-24-12 (R-O-U-R)
• Week 9	MWF	Total Throws 78	13-26-26-13 (R-O-U-R)

Player Workout Guide: Velocity Development Protocol:*

KEYS TO INCREASING A PLAYER'S THROWING VELOCITY
Since throwing velocity is a critical skill for the success of a baseball player (no matter what position is being played), it is important for each player to develop this skill to his maximum potential. Training with underweight and overweight implements has been proven to increase the throwing velocity of throwing athletes.

* © Decker Sports, LLC; One Decker Place; 6912 N. 97th Circle; Omaha, Nebraska 68122

❑ Theory:

The first principle underlying baseball velocity training is the understanding that throwing is a ballistic action. Throwing involves rapid, explosive movements, requiring specific types of training. The ability to produce these explosive movements is greatly influenced by the percentage of type IIB (fast-twitch) muscle fibers contained within an athlete's muscle cells. In order to produce more rapid and forceful contractions of these fast-twitch muscle fibers, training must be done at 100% intensity (game speed). Traditional weight training with machines or free-weights, while performing non-specific slow movements, will not increase the throwing velocity of athletes who already possess a baseline level of strength. In fact, some research has shown that prolonged heavy, non-specific weight training may actually reduce movement speeds.

Training with underweight and overweight implements has its roots in the speed and strength specificity-training programs of track and field athletes in the former Soviet-bloc countries. The results from research conducted with these athletes indicated several insightful points, including: employing variable weighted-training implements enhances power development; variations of weighted-training implements should range between 5 and 20% of "normal" (competition) weight; and a 2:1 frequency ratio of throwing (2 weighted: 1 normal) maximized power output. By throwing underweight baseballs, body segments will move at higher speeds with less muscle force. When throwing overweight balls, body segments travel at slower speeds, but with greater force. Thus, underweight training can be referred to as speed training, and overweight training as strength training. Power is defined as speed times strength. Because of the ballistic nature of throwing, safely training the body to develop the greatest amount of power in the least amount of time during this sport-specific movement is critical for the development of throwing velocity.

❑ Research:

In April 2000, a team of researchers from the Michael W. Krzyzewski Human Performance Laboratory at Duke University and the American Sports Medicine Institute in Birmingham, Alabama, reviewed all of the existing research concerning the effects of throwing underweight and overweight balls (Escamilla, et al., *Sports Med 2000*; Apr; 29 (4): 259-272). Escamilla, et al. reviewed 11 overweight- and underweight-studies (lasting 6-to-12 weeks in duration) that were conducted during the athletes' off-season.

Data from these studies "strongly support the practice of training with overweight and underweight baseballs to increase throwing velocity of regulation baseballs." All but one of the studies reported significant increases in throwing velocity by the underweight- and/or overweight-ball experimental groups. Six of the studies reviewed contained control groups that involved participants who threw *only regulation balls (load ball or game-implement weight)* during the experiment. None of the control groups experienced significant increases in throwing velocity. Based on this data, Escamilla et al.

concluded: "From most of the research now available on weighted-implement throwing, it appears that the ideal weight of overweight and underweight balls is within 20% of the weight of a regulation baseball. Hence, underweight baseballs should weigh between four and five ounces, while overweight baseballs should weigh between five and six ounces." (Accordingly, the weight of softballs should 5.2 ounces, 6.5 ounces, and 7.8 ounces, respectively.)

While these studies focused on the effects of baseball training, their results can be easily extrapolated to softball. Athletes (with the exception of pitchers) in each sport use an identical overhand throwing motion. Furthermore, at the moment of front-foot strike, baseball and softball pitchers are in a nearly identical position. The differences occur as the pitcher delivers the ball to the hitter. However, both movements—underhand pitching and overhand pitching—are extremely rapid and forceful. Thus, the same principles of training these similar, distinctive movements are applicable to each other.

❏ Training Protocol:
Decker Sports strongly suggests the following procedures be followed when implementing underweight/overweight throwing training:
- Proper warm-up of core body temperature
- Sport-specific flexibility exercises
- Pre-training warm-up with the regulation weight ball (load) throwing at less than 100% intensity

Once these steps are completed, the training protocol may begin. In that regard, Tables 12-2 amd 12-3 detail the off-season training schedules that Coop DeRenne employed in training pitchers. It is recommended that either of these schedules be used:

R = 5-oz. ball   U = 4-oz. ball   O = 6-oz. ball

❏ Important Points:
- Throwing distances for any player should not exceed either 150 feet or a distance that a ball can be thrown on a line-drive trajectory with proper mechanics.
- Pitchers have three options: throw from the regulation pitching distance off of a standard mound, throwing all fastballs with proper mechanics; pitch from the regulation pitching distance off of flat ground; or use the long-toss protocol up to 150 feet.
- *All* athletes should make each throw during training sessions at 100% intensity.

While research supports the notion that training with overweight and underweight balls enhances throwing velocity, all of the studies were conducted during the off-season. For the following reasons, it seems appropriate to continue training in-season as well:

- No injuries were reported during any of the studies.
- By limiting the variance of ball weights to 20%, it appears that throwing mechanics are not altered.
- All players typically lose strength, and consequently throwing velocity, throughout the in-season period.

Weeks	No. of Sessions	Total Throws	Sequence of Throws
1-2	3	54	9-18-18-9 (R-O-U-R)
3-4	3	60	10-20-20-10 (R-O-U-R)
5-6	3	66	11-22-22-11 (R-O-U-R)
7-8	3	72	12-24-24-12 (R-O-U-R)
9-10	3	78	13-26-26-13 (R-O-U-R)
		OR	
1-2	3	54	9-36-9 (R-O- R)
3-4	3	60	10-40-10 (R-O-R)
5	3	66	11-44-11 (R-O-R)
6	3	66	11-44-44 (R-U-R)
7-8	3	72	12-48-12 (R-U-R)
9-10	3	78	13-52-13 (R-U-R)

Table 12-2. Off-season training schedule—option A

Weeks	No. of Sessions	Total Throws	Sequence of Throws
1-3	2	60	10-20-20-10 (R-O-U-R)
4-6	2	54	9-18-18-9 (R-O-U-R)
7-9	2	48	8-16-16-8 (R-O-U-R)
10-12	2	42	7-14-14-7 (R-O-U-R)
13-15	2	36	6-12-12-6 (R-O-U-R)

Table 12-3. Off-season training schedule—option B

ALL players, regardless of position, should adhere to the protocols outlined in Tables 12-2 and 12-3. The focus of the in-season protocol should be to maintain throwing velocity.

❏ Note:

Because all of the research regarding throwing underweight and overweight baseballs was conducted with high school and college-age athletes, Decker Sports does not recommend the use of the overload ball (six ounce) for athletes under the age of 14, until further research is undertaken and the findings of such investigative efforts confirm that it is appropriate for athletes of al ages. For athletes under 14 years of age, use of the protocol throwing the underload ball (four ounce) and standard load ball (five ounce) is recommended. Proper adult supervision with a coach or professional trainer should always be employed when performing the protocol. It should be noted that Decker Sports assumes no liability for any injury that may occur while throwing or catching baseballs of any weight.

13

Summary of the 2005-2006 Velocity Study

(Tom House and Eric Andrews)

Actions After the Research Was Gathered and Analyzed

Once the data had been collected, we had to decide what to do with it. To our knowledge, no similar study had ever been done in this manner, and we were excited to learn something new, especially something that goes against such widespread conventional wisdom. With our findings, we hypothesized that we could improve a pitcher's velocity with improved hip and shoulder separation. We felt the best way to respond to these findings was to design drills specifically to improve pitchers in this area, but more importantly, to design a strength and flexibility program for pitchers to get them stronger and more flexible in their core and torso. In our opinion, such an approach would enable our pitchers to increase their hip/shoulder separation, getting it closer to a more efficient angle of 60 degrees, thus allowing them to throw harder.

We then created a pilot study called the SUV Program (Safe Usable Velocity Improvement Program). We used the information from our research during the summer to work with a group of 23 local high school varsity players from the San Diego area. In addition to having the pitchers work out with our trainer on a weekly basis, the players also threw heavy/light baseballs (overloading/underloading with six-ounce and four-ounce baseballs) under our supervision on a weekly basis. To help build strength and increase arm speed, the number of weighted-ball throwing days varied among players. The entire program lasted 12 weeks. The results of the program are detailed in Tables 13-1 to 13-3 and Charts 13-1 to 13-2.

A brief description of the SUV Program includes the following:

- Players came in for an initial assessment where we recorded their velocities for the first time. We also measured each player's angle of hip/shoulder separation (from the knee position) to learn his efficiency at that particular point in time.
- Players came in once a week to work out with our trainer. In addition to participating in the workouts that evolved and increased in workloads/repetitions/types of exercises over the 12 weeks, the players were given packets each week that demonstrated the exact exercises they were to do on their own throughout the week. Players performed the individual workouts up to five times a week on their own. Records for each player were kept indicating how many times they did their homework each week away from our supervision.
- Players also came into the facility once a week to throw under the supervision of an NPA instructor.
- Depending on the player's current game and practice schedule (throwing routine), the players either threw the weighted balls or participated in a normal bullpen session to focus on mechanics.
- The velocities of every pitch thrown by each pitcher during each individual workout were recorded. Most workouts consisted of:
  ✓ 10 velocities with a six-ounce baseball
  ✓ 10 velocities with a four-ounce baseball
  ✓ 10 velocities with a standard Major League five-ounce baseball
- By keeping detailed velocity records for each pitcher, we were able to measure the progress/digress of each pitcher. A summary sheet after the study was completed provided the following information:
  ✓ The velocity of every pitch thrown with each baseball
  ✓ Averages, modes, spreads, percentages, maximums, and minimums to track their progress/digress
  ✓ Which week during the program (one through 12) the players had the best/least improvement from their initial assessment
- Though not the central goal of our research, the results of the SUV program indicated that the optimal number of individual workouts per athlete was approximately three workouts per week. Continued research on this topic should be conducted to provide a more accurate assessment of the relationship between pitch velocity and workout frequency.

NPA SUV STUDY FINAL DATA

Name: Pitcher # 1

DATE	AGE	LEVEL	BUILD
# of weeks throwing	# of workouts attended	Best week avg/best top speed	Ball weight
10	12	10/10	6 oz / 4 oz / 5 oz

Velocity from Mound

DATE	Ball Weight	1	2	3	4	5	6	7	8	9	10	Top	Average
11/15/05	6	69	69	71	70	70	69	70	70	69	70	71	70
	4	79	76	79	79	75	79	75	78	77	77	79	77
	5	74	74	74	74	72	75	76	76	75	74	76	74
11/21/05	6	68	70	68	71	71	70	72	71	70	71	72	70
	4	76	78	79	78	78	80	78	79	76	77	80	78
	5	75	76	72	73	74	74	73	75	74	75	76	74
12/6/05	6	71	71	71	72	71	71	72	71	71	73	73	71
	4	79	81	79	81	76	79	81	80	80	83	83	80
	5	78	75	78	70	79	78	73	77	73	80	80	76
12/12/05	6	72	73	72	72	71	72	72	72	72	72	73	72
	4	79	79	78	81	81	80	79	80	82	82	82	80
	5	79	77	79	79	77	77	78	78	78	80	80	78
12/19/05	6	69	70	70	70	70	69	70	72	71	70	72	70
	4	78	76	78	81	79	79	79	79	78	81	81	79
	5	72	77	73	76	73	75	76	73	72	71	76	74
12/26/05	6	70	70	70	71	71	72	72	71	72	72	72	71
	4	83	80	79	79	78	79	80	81	82	80	83	80
	5	78	77	76	76	76	76	75	77	77	76	78	76
1/9/06	6	69	68	69	68	68	68	67	67	70	70	70	68
	4	82	80	81	80	81	82	83	81	81	84	84	82
	5	77	78	76	79	77	79	78	80	79	79	80	78
1/16/06	6	71	72	74	71	72	72	72	74	73	73	74	72
	4	79	81	81	81	80	82	81	81	82	81	82	81
	5	75	79	80	77	77	78	78	78	81	81	81	78
1/23/06	6	71	73	71	71	71	71	72	71	73	72	73	72
	4	82	82	81	81	82	81	81	83	81	84	84	82
	5	78	77	77	76	77	75	78	76	77	77	78	77
2/14/06	6	71	72	72	74	71						74	72
	4	84	84	82	82	83	84					84	83
	5	79	82	82	78	80	80	81	81	81	80	82	81

First Weighted Ball Session (AVG)	Last Weighted Ball Session (AVG)	Best Weighted Ball (Top Speed)	Delta from first to last	Delta from first to best	Initial FB Average Velocity	Best Average Velocity during Program	Delta	Initial FB Top Velocity	Best Velocity during Program	Delta
70	72	74	+2	+4						
77	83	84	+6	+7						
74	80	82	+6	+8	74	80	+6	76	82	+6

Table 13-1. Test results from the 2005-2006 velocity study

Summary of Progress for Pitchers 1 - 23								
Initial vs Best Average Velocity Improvement					Initial vs Best Velocity Improvement (top speed)			
0 - 1 mph	2 - 3 mph	4 - 5 mph	6 mph and up		0 - 1 mph	2 - 3 mph	4 - 5 mph	6 mph and up
4	11	4	4		4	5	5	9
(number of pitchers per category)					(number of pitchers per category)			

Table 13-2. Summary of progress achieved by pitchers

Ratio of best week AVG velocity vs # of workouts attended			Ratio of best week TOP velocity vs # of workouts attended	
Pitcher	Ratio		Pitcher	Ratio
1	100%		1	100%
2	100%		2	100%
3	25%		3	25%
4	67%		4	67%
5	100%		5	100%
6	50%		6	50%
7	75%		7	75%
8	33%		8	33%
9	100%		9	100%
10	90%		10	90%
11	71%		11	57%
12	100%		12	100%
13	67%		13	16%
14	100%		14	100%
15	25%		15	25%
16	50%		16	50%
17	100%		17	90%
18	100%		18	80%
19	100%		19	100%
20	80%		20	80%
21	67%		21	67%
22	100%		22	78%
23	33%		23	33%

Table 13-3. Velocity ratio summary data

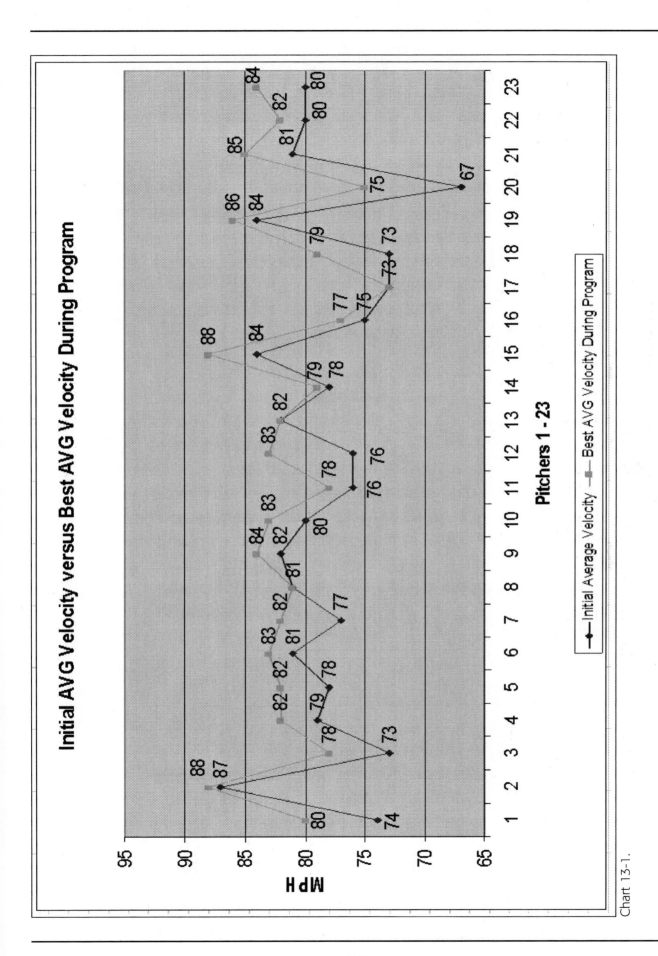

Chart 13-1.

Chart 13-2.

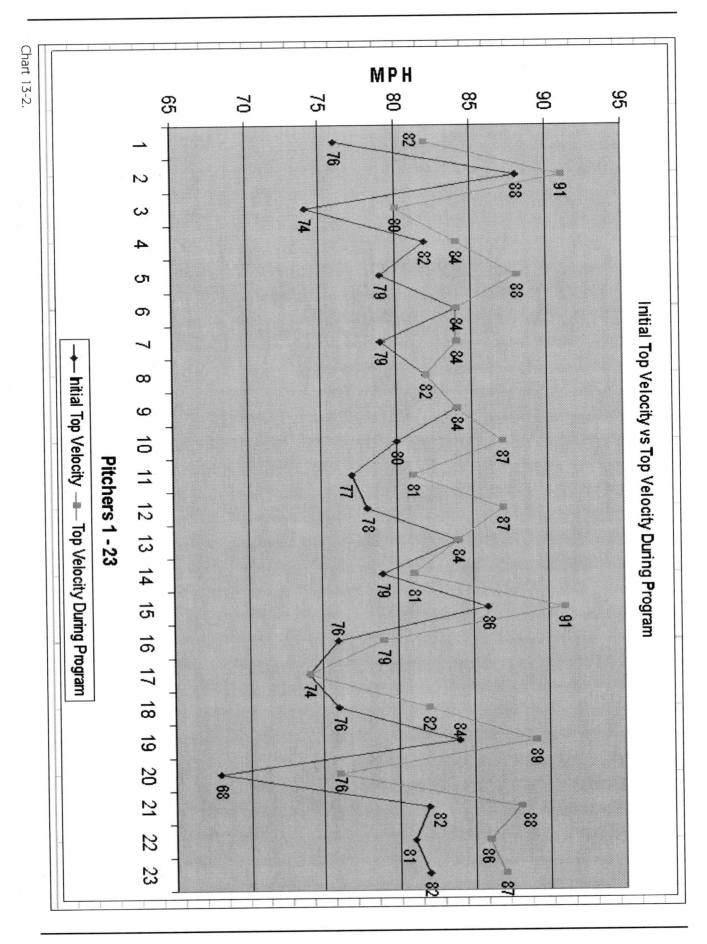

Initial Top Velocity vs Top Velocity During Program

MPH

Pitchers 1 - 23

Initial Top Velocity —■— Top Velocity During Program

CONCLUSIONS AND RECOMMENDATIONS

It is important to remember that essentially our research primarily involved a series of preliminary studies that should, hopefully, generate enough "buzz" to motivate others to prove, disprove, and/or improve our real-velocity findings. The following are the conclusions and recommendations of our research to date:

- Eighty percent of a pitcher's real velocity comes from rotational momentum if his kinematic sequencing and energy translation are efficient.
- Twenty percent of a pitcher's real velocity comes from directional momentum if his kinematic sequencing and energy translation are efficient.
- All pitchers have their unique interpretation of a universal biomechanical signature; they just look differently doing the same things.
- It's easier to alter the timing of this signature than it is to change the signature. Timing is getting a pitcher to the right place at the right time with the right kinematic sequence.
- Biomechanical inefficiencies are minimized when there is less time in a pitcher's weight transfer. With less time, fewer things can go wrong.
- The less functional strength/flexibility a pitcher has, the less time a pitcher should take in his weight transfer. Less time requires less strength.
- Training the total body to move fast when throwing/pitching teaches efficient timing and sequencing.
- Biomechanically training scapular loading involves movement and strength recruitment out of sequence, which alters kinematic sequencing and energy translation, sub-optimizes real velocity, and increases the risk of injury.
- Strength training scapular loading for rotational stability is essential.
- Strength training the core for rotational stability is important.

- Pitchers are only as strong as their weakest biomechanical/physical link.
- Pitchers will find that their posture, stride length, and arm path length will be whatever their bodies are strong enough to support.
- Fastball velocity is optimized when pitchers match their mechanical efficiency cross-specific functional strength, stability, mobility, and flexibility with fast-twitch neuromuscular enhancement.
- If strength/endurance training protocols do not facilitate/enhance extremity/core stability, mobility, and flexibility, then they are detracting from performance/health.

Finally, baseball should increase its effort to research and develop more functional, cross-specific "rotational" training protocols for pitchers of all ages and skill levels. We had fun writing *Fastball Fitness* and hope you enjoyed reading it.

Yours in baseball,
Tom House

Ludewig PM, Cook TM. Alterations in shoulder kinematics and associated muscle activity in people with symptoms of shoulder impingements. *Physical Therapy*, 80(3): pp. 276-291, 2000.

Matsuo T, Escamilla RF, Fleisig GS, Barrentine SW, Andrews JF. Comparison of kinematic and temporal parameters between different pitch velocity groups. *Journal of Applied Biomechanics*, 17(1): 1-13, 2001.

Mileski RA, Snyder SJ. Superior labral lesions in the shoulder: pathoanatomy and surgical management. *J AM Academy Orthopedic Surgery*, 6: 121-131, 1998.

Moseley JB, Jobe FW, Pink M, Perry J, Tibone J. EMG analysis of the scapular muscles during a shoulder rehabilitation program. *Am J Sports Med*, 20(2): pp. 128-134, 1992.

Stodden DF, Fleisig GS, McLean SP, Andrews JR. Relationship of Biomechanical Factors to Baseball Pitching Velocity: Within Pitcher Variation. *Journal of Applied Biomechanics*, 21(1): 44-56, 2005.

Stodden DF, Fleisig GS, McLean SP, Lyman SL, Andrews JR. Relationship of pelvis and upper torso kinematics to pitched baseball velocity. *Journal of Applied Biomechanics*, 17(2): 164-172, 2001.

Unpublished study: DeRenne/House Diamond Baseball (1987-88); over/underloading using six-, five-, and four-ounce baseballs; involved 41 high school pitchers and 70 university-level pitchers

Unpublished study: House/Andrews/NPA/Decker Sports (2005-06); over/underloading using six-, five-, and four-ounce baseballs; involved 23 high school pitchers

Unpublished study: Coach Steve Russell, Omaha Central High School/NPA/Decker Sports (2004); over/underloading using six- five- and four-ounce baseballs; involved eight high school pitchers

Vasiliev, LA, Use of different weights to develop specialized speed strength. *Soviet Sports Review*, 18(1): 49-52, 1983.

Suggested References

About the Contributors

Tom House, Ph.D.

Considered by many to be the "father of modern pitching mechanics," Tom House is the co-founder of the National Pitching Association. The NPA is renowned for its efforts involving three-dimensional analysis of human movement, the physical preparation to support this movement, the metabolic preparation to fuel human activity, and the necessary mental and emotional make-up to successfully achieve the highest level of performance possible. Tom pitched on the professional level from 1967 to 1979 for the Atlanta Braves, Boston Red Sox, and Seattle Mariners. He has coached since 1980 for the Houston Astros, San Diego Padres, Texas Rangers, and Chiba Lotte Marines (Japan), as well as in Latin America. On the amateur level, Tom is an information and instruction coordinator for 12 baseball academies across the United States and Canada. He directly accesses 8,000-10,000 players, coaches, and parents per year in clinic settings. He travels the world as an international consultant, performance analyst, and sports psychologist. Tom is currently an advisor with the American Sports Medicine Institute and the Titleist Performance Institute, was a co-founder of the Pitch It Forward Foundation, and has paneled seminars for the American College of Sports Medicine.

Eric Andrews

Eric Andrews is in his eleventh year working with Tom House and is one of the three members of the NPA coaching staff at the NPA Performance Center and Motion Lab in San Diego. In addition to instructing pitchers at the facility, Eric is responsible for marketing NPA products and services, conducting research on and off the field, and developing new opportunities and experiences nationwide for members of the NPA family. In addition to his efforts with the NPA, Eric manages two youth baseball teams in Del Mar, California. Over the past seven seasons, his Del Mar Tigers have won four state championships, and his teams have held high national rankings throughout their existence. Eric is also passionate about coaching at the high school level and has coached the last several years at both University City and Mission Bay high schools in San Diego.

Eric Barajas, MA, CSCS

Eric Barajas is a highly regarded personal trainer and top producer for the prestigious Pacific Athletic Club of San Diego. His areas of expertise include rotational athletic movement. He has extensive experience working with both MLB and NFL athletes. Eric also trains numerous athletes at the collegiate level in a variety of sports. He is renowned for providing his clients with innovative exercises to help them reach their fitness goals in a comfortable and fun environment.

Troy M. Merckle, PT, CSCS

Troy Merckle is a licensed physical therapist who works in an orthopedic setting, focusing specifically on rehabilitating sports-related injuries. Troy is a graduate of The Ohio State University and has been certified as a Strength and Conditioning Specialist by the National Strength and Conditioning Association (NSCA). He has served as a consultant with both the Cincinnati Reds and the Washington Nationals, for which he has been to spring training for the past several years, evaluating athletes and designing both rehab and conditioning programs. Merckle has assisted with NFL combine evaluations and training, as well as designing training programs for sports such as volleyball, soccer, basketball, wrestling, track and field, softball, and lacrosse. Troy has also worked closely with several gymnasts from the Cincinnati Gymnastics Academy.

Mike Paul

Mike Paul has been training pitchers for more than two decades. A partner in Elite Baseball & Softball Training in Grand Rapids, Michigan, Mike is responsible for the development of the pitching program and the overall health/strength training regimen for the entire Elite program. Mike has trained 16 pitchers who have signed professionally, in addition to over 100 individuals who have subsequently received opportunities to play collegiately. For the past 11 years, he has scouted for the Minnesota Twins. Mike and his wife, Michelle, have three children, Michael, Stacey and Cannon.

Greg Rose, D.C.

Greg Rose is a board-certified Doctor of Chiropractic and holds an undergraduate degree in engineering from the University of Maryland. Greg specializes in 3-D biomechanics, strength and conditioning, manual therapy, rehabilitation, nutritional supplementation, and therapeutic exercises for golf. Over the past eight years, he has helped over 500 professional golfers and 3,000 amateurs reach their peak performance through physical conditioning and nutritional support. His unique form of functional training, combined with golf-specific motor learning drills, has made him one of the top strength and conditioning coaches for golf in the United States. Greg currently resides in Oceanside, CA and is the co-founder of the new Titleist Performance Institute. Greg is also the president and founder of Clubgolf Fitness Center in Gaithersburg, MD, the largest golf-specific health club in the United States.

Alan Tyson, PT, SCS, ATC-L, CSCS

Alan Tyson is vice president of sports performance and rehabilitation for OrthoCarolina. He is a physical therapist, board-certified as a sports clinical specialist. He is also a certified athletic trainer, as well as a certified strength and conditioning specialist. He worked several years with the Charlotte Knights (AAA affiliate for the Chicago White Sox) and continues to serve as a consultant to the team. Alan is also a consultant with the Carolina Panthers, Charlotte Sting, and Charlotte Eagles. Alan is the co-developer of Jumpmetrics—a jump-training and performance program for female athletes and also has founded two pitching programs designed to increase velocity and decrease arm injuries. Alan has spoken regionally and nationally about numerous rehabilitative topics and is also the column editor of "Rehab Tips" for the *National Strength and Conditioning Journal*.

Simon Webb

Simon Webb is an exercise scientist who has been training athletes across a number of individual and team sports, ranging from junior-to-elite professionals, since 1996. He is currently employed at the Victorian Institute of Sport in Australia as a strength and conditioning coach, assisting athletes from various sports as they train for Olympic and Commonwealth Games, world championships, and international and domestic competition. He specializes in designing strength and conditioning programs for rotational-based sports, including golf and tennis.